BATH AND WELLS
A Diocesan Celebration

Robert Dunning

ryelands

First published in Great Britain in 2008
Reprinted 2009

Copyright © 2008 Robert Dunning

British Library Cataloguing-in-Publication Data
A CIP record for this title is available from the British Library

ISBN 978 0 9556477 8 9

RYELANDS
Halsgrove House,
Ryelands Industrial Estate,
Bagley Road, Wellington, Somerset TA21 9PZ
Tel: 01823 653777   Fax: 01823 216796
email: sales@halsgrove.com

Part of the Halsgrove group of companies
Information on all Halsgrove titles is available at: www.halsgrove.com

Printed and bound by Grafiche Flaminia, Italy

Contents

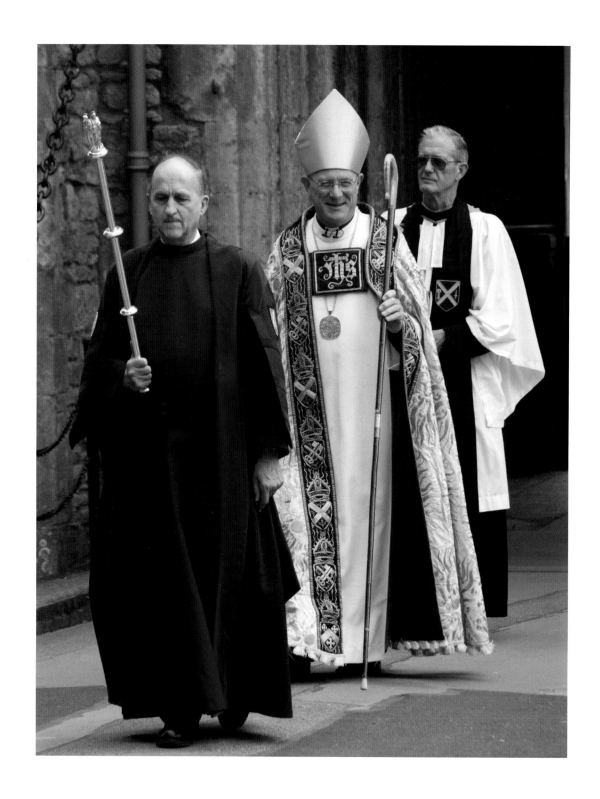

Acknowledgements

In December 2005 the Diocesan Secretary, Nick Denison, first made the suggestion that a history might be produced to mark the 1100th anniversary of the founding of the diocese of what is now called Bath and Wells. The award of a grant by the Viscount Amory Trust, the willing co-operation of publisher Steven Pugsley and the skill of the designers Karen Binaccioni and Sharon O'Inn are here acknowledged with thanks. The Revd Eric Illing, the Ven John Burgess, formerly archdeacon of Bath, and Jon Rose helpfully commented on parts of the text. Michael Blandford, Anne Crawford and Jean Moore of Wells Cathedral, Helen Garrett of the Bishop's Palace, Cathryn Spence, Paul Garayo and Sonia Roe of the Public Catalogue Foundation, David Bromwich of the Somerset Archaeological and Natural History Society, Matthew Clements of Glastonbury Abbey, John Page, Hugh and Bridget Playfair and Jerry Sampson have all been most helpful in providing illustrations, some at very short notice. Frances Neale has given permission for the use of photographs by her late husband Richard. Ownership of images is acknowledged in appropriate captions and implies permission to publish; those in black-and-white by Phil Day were commissioned by the Templar Trust to illustrate a year in the life of the diocese. My wife Anne has endured papers scattered in apparent disorder in various parts of our home, has allowed me the temporary use of her digital camera and has provided much-needed technical assistance with the results.

Robert Dunning
Pentecost 2008

Opposite page: *Peter Price leaving the Palace for his enthronement in his cathedral, 12 May 2002.*

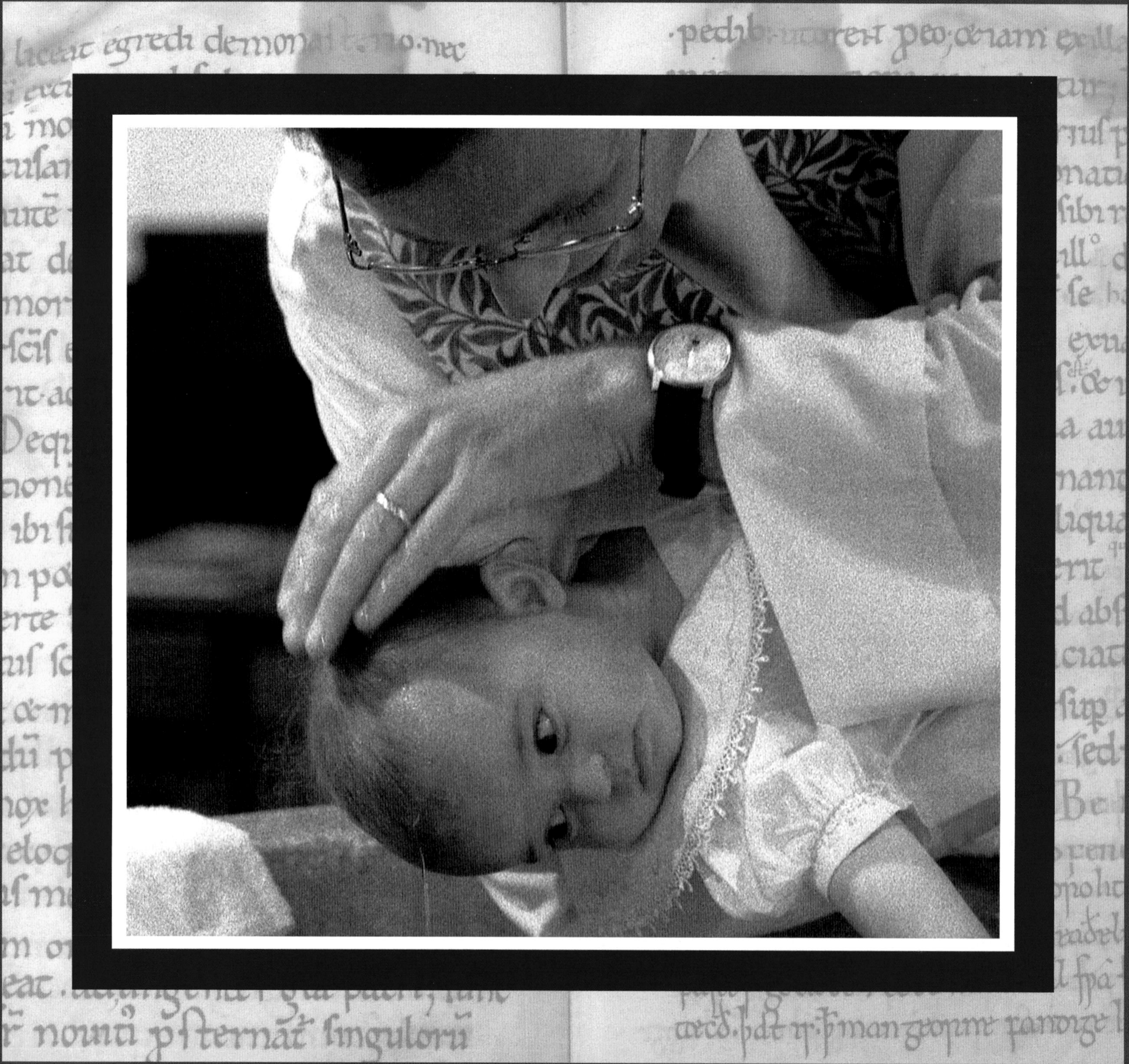

1

In the Beginning

Genesis 1.1

Northover church on its knoll overlooking Ilchester's Roman cemetery. A minster until the eleventh century. Robert Dunning

hristians had long been living and worshipping in what came to be Somerset when its people were given their own bishop in 909. How long is impossible to tell precisely, though the legends told to pilgrims visiting Glastonbury at the end of the twelfth century claimed that Jesus himself had visited the place and that Joseph of Arimathea had been sent there by the Apostle Philip forty years after the Crucifixion.

That kind of history will not do for the sceptical twenty-first century, and there are those who think that the cross that was found in the Roman cemetery beside the Fosse Way at Shepton Mallet is a clever forgery. What cannot be questioned is the Christian symbol in the Roman mosaic floor just over the Dorset border at Hinton St Mary, clear evidence that the message of the gospel had reached a country landowner in our part of England. And what would make very good sense is that among the many visitors to the popular Roman city of Aquae Sulis from all over the empire should have been Christians who, after all, would have found its healing waters as helpful for their physical ills as for the ills of any unbeliever. There may well, too, have been businessmen or visitors at Ilchester when it was a busy Roman town, but only the excavation of the cemetery on its northern edge beneath Northover church will reveal the truth.

And the position of Northover church is a more positive clue to the likelihood of Christian Romans in Somerset, for it was one of those churches (however small and forlorn it seems now) that, like Banwell, Bruton, Cheddar and Keynsham, were in or very near Roman settlements and became important at the time of the conversion of the Saxons. All came to be mission centres because a Christian tradition had been kept alive.

How far groups of converts were part of a recognisably organised church when the Roman Empire still held power is impossible to say, but several British bishops were summoned to meetings on the continent at least twice in the early years of the fourth century and are likely to have

Opposite page:
In the Beginning. Phil Day 2004
(© Templar Trust)

been based in cities on the Roman pattern. At the same time Christian groups following a British or Celtic tradition clearly survived in the west of Britain.

THE CONVERSION OF THE PEOPLE

Ever since King Ethelbert of Kent listened to St Augustine after his arrival from Rome in 597 and became convinced of his message, the conversion of the English people was brought about through the conversion of kings. Cynegils, the first Christian West Saxon king (611—?642), was baptised in 635, but already the countryside he and his men gradually occupied was dotted with misson churches, some later known as minsters, that were served by priests living together in community.

Their traditions were probably not those Cynegils adopted from his Rome-appointed bishop Birinus of Dorchester (Oxon), but rather those so stoutly defended by the bishops and teachers Augustine had confronted twice at Aust some years before. There the monk from Rome had played the role of Elijah before the priests of Baal, proving the rightness of his cause by restoring sight to a blind man, but still failing to convince seven Celtic bishops and many scholars that the Roman way of calculating Easter, the Roman rite of baptism and a common mission to the Saxons ('the nation of the English') was the best way forward. The traditionalists, for their part, did not care for what they saw as a dominating bishop completely lacking in necessary humility.

King Cenwealh (642—672), succeeding his father as ruler of the West Saxons and evidently acting with the approval of Archbishop Theodore of Canterbury (669—690), accepted those mission churches of the native tradition but concentrated especially on Sherborne, Glastonbury and Exeter, confirming to them the land they already held to support their clergy. Centwine, Cenwealh's son, in 678 declared in a charter that he had appointed an abbot to Glastonbury on the advice of Haedde, bishop of Winchester. Those three British Christian centres were thus brought in some way into the orbit of the emerging state and also by that time within the diocese of Winchester. At about the same time the monastery at Bath was founded by Osric, king of the neighbouring Hwicce, the people of the later kingdom of Mercia.

Ine (688—726) and his successors as kings of Wessex continued their support of the church, increasing the wealth of Glastonbury and founding churches at Wells and Muchelney. Ine's decision to make the monastery at Sherborne the seat of a bishop to be responsible for the western half of the by now unmanageable bishopric of Winchester brought to power and influence the great missionary Bishop Aldhelm, founder of communities at Frome, Bruton and probably Doulting. Frithogyth, wife of Ine's successor Aethelheard, founded a minster at Taunton.

How far was this missionary effort successful? The laws of the West Saxon kings from Ine onwards are concerned as much with the church as the state. Ine's laws, compiled with the advice of his father Cenred and his bishops Haedde of Winchester and Eorcenwold of London and discussed at 'a great assembly of the servants of God', inevitably concentrated on criminal

Part of a ninth-century cross, West Camel. Hugh and Bridget Playfair

Sanctuary ring, Baltonsborough.
Robert Dunning

behaviour and its consequences; but there were also laws insisting on the necessity of baptism, about not working on Sundays, paying church taxes, and offering temporary sanctuary in a church building to a criminal in flight. That last right was claimed in 1319 by Bishop Droxford when a man was dragged from Chedzoy church to Somerton gaol still holding the door-ring which he trusted would have saved him. Bishop Droxford demanded him back from the king's officers by citing the ancient law. Other laws emphasised the sanctity of a minster as a place of peace, referred to communicants, godfathers and godsons, and the rite of confirmation.

King Alfred, king 871-99, made reference to Ine's laws when making his own code in those years after peace had been made with the Danes, and they were still relatively new when Wells diocese was formed. Under them a bishop could impose penance on offenders willing to receive it; and those who were not were sentenced to outlawry and excommunication, the shutting out 'from all the churches of Christ'. Theft, according to Alfred's code, was twice as bad if committed on Sundays, at Christmas, Easter, or during Lent; and the state was prepared to enforce the church's Lenten rules with fines. One law even accepted the possibility that a priest might commit murder, for which he was to be unfrocked by his bishop and pay his entire income in compensation.

King Alfred not only expected his bishops to see his laws were carried out; he also expected them to teach, and actually provided him with a textbook, a copy of his own translation of a book by Pope Gregory the Great on the subject of pastoral care. Bishops would thus gather a group of clergy together, place the book on some kind of stand so that all could see, and read and study it line by line with the use of a pointer. That pointer, perhaps of ivory or wood, was valuable, in recognition of the significance of both the book and the subject, for the country had only recently been ravaged by the Danes, churches laid waste, and pastors scattered. Restoration of church life was vital, so the end of the pointer the bishop held was deliberately elaborate and valuable, provided by the king himself. The bishop would be in no doubt of the importance of his teaching, his listeners in no doubt of the importance of the words they were studying and the task that lay ahead of them. One of those valuable pointer-handles, known technically as an aestel, lost like all the others, was found at the end of the seventeenth century just outside North Petherton and has become known as the Alfred Jewel. It is an amazing piece of jewellery, made partly of gold fashioned on the continent, partly of crystal almost certainly originating in a Roman mansion on the Adriatic. Its name, most appropriately, has been adopted for the parishes around North Petherton that now work and learn and worship together.

The Alfred Jewel, found near North Petherton in 1694. Ashmolean Museum, Oxford

But for all the bishops, laws and textbooks, how deep was the conversion of the people? Clues are few and far between, and people cling to traditions, even in the twenty-first century, not realising that some of them are pagan. In the early eleventh century all priests were encouraged to stop paganism including, as their instructions explained, 'the nonsense which is performed on New Year's Day' and they were to discourage heathen songs and the devil's games on feast days. The puritans made similar complaints in the early seventeenth century. In Somerset a spot on Ilminster's estate boundary and another at Priston was called 'the ford of the pagans' in late Saxon times, a name which stuck for several hundred years and was no doubt used by people converted from such beliefs. In the mid ninth century, two hundred years and more after the coming of the Christian Saxons, some still thought of an ash tree on the boundary of Halse as sacred, though the description of that boundary made clear that most thought they were ignorant. Ash and apple trees feature commonly as boundary markers in documents still being copied long after the Norman Conquest, and a place at Batcombe was still recalled as 'the sacred place of the wood'. And there was a 'holy' spring at Ruishton in the ninth century and another just outside Taunton that gave its name to Wilton, neither proof of real holiness. The evidence for individual conversions in Saxon England is hard to come by outside the experiences of famous saints, and saints in Somerset are scarce; but church regulations issued from time to time in the tenth and elevnth centuries, while acknowledging the need for the faith to be taught, the services understood, saints honoured and church and clergy supported, made clear that it was lay folk who were in constant

Pagan guardians of the church? Three faces look down from the tower buttress, Stratton on the Fosse. Robert Dunning

need of correction because of poor attendance at services, lax Sunday observance, and improper behaviour in church, where talking, drinking or eating 'foolishly' was clearly common and where dogs, horses and particularly pigs were to be found wandering, and worse, in churchyards.

A NEW DIOCESE

Perhaps seeing the need to strengthen the government of his fast-expanding kingdom, Alfred's son Edward the Elder made the decision, presumably with the advice of his bishops, to divide the huge area looked after by the bishop of Sherborne. It was a convenient moment, for Sherborne had recently been left fatherless by the death of Bishop Asser and had clearly become too large and too populous for one man's responsibility. The solution was to divide it into three parts; Devon was given its own bishop, to be based at Crediton, Dorset was to remain with Asser's successor at Sherborne. The third part, Somerset, had for some years been under the care of a bishop named Esne working in and around Taunton. So the people of Somerset were given their own bishop as part of a move to more localised administration.

The choice of Athelm as Somerset's first bishop brought a man who was probably then a monk at Glastonbury but was also a member of a local aristocratic family. He was presumably the king's choice, and Wells as his base of operations was possibly a matter of circumstance, since both Wells and Glastonbury owed much to the king's ancestor Ine. Perhaps it was felt that Athelm could hardly remain at Glastonbury where he was not abbot but the decision for the minster church at Wells as his cathedral was to prove for many years to come unfortunate. The two close neighbours could never be bosom friends.

Across the new diocese under the leadership of Bishop Athelm a body of clergy ministered to the people of Somerset, a people identified in the Anglo-Saxon Chronicle for their successful support of King Alfred, a Christian king fighting for survival against pagan invaders. Alfred, in founding monasteries at Athelney and Shaftesbury, declared that religious life had disappeared during those troubled times, meaning probably the community life that had existed in the minsters. But Athelm arrived as bishop after thirty years of reconstruction when at least some of them had recovered their endowments and their mission purpose. How many there were is impossible to say; some may have suffered more than others from the theft of treasures, the destruction of buildings and the scattering of their clergy. Glastonbury, Taunton, Bruton, Muchelney, Keynsham and Bath recovered enough to become, in time, home to communities of monks or canons that survived for the next six hundred years, Wells for even longer. Cheddar and Banwell lost their status as religious communities and both became part of the bishop's property, though Banwell retained two satellites, Puxton and Churchill, which seem to have originated as daughters founded by its mission priests.

And there were other minsters, later surrounded by clusters of daughters, which show how

St Decuman's well: a new and safe site for the old minster.
Robert Dunning

they spread the gospel in their immediate neighbourhoods and were at the same time closely linked with units of secular administration called hundreds. They probably emerged in the years when the West Saxon state was being consolidated in the later years of the eighth century. Among them were Chewton (Mendip) with two daughters at Easton and others at Farrington, Paulton and Emborough; South Petherton with at least Barrington, Chillington, Lopen and Seavington St Mary, and Crewkerne with Mi(n)sterton, Seaborough, Wayford and Eastham. The minster of St Decuman, formerly on the crumbling cliff-top west of Watchet and removed to a safer site across the valley, was still a religious community under a dean in the mid twelfth century. Its chapel at Williton still acknowledged its ancient dependence in 1412 when its people agreed to attend the parish church on Ascension Day, on the day of its dedication and on the feast of the translation of St Decuman. Memories of such links lasted a long time: the people of Wayford were still offering the key of their church on Crewkerne's high altar in the 1830s.

Reformers two centuries on wanted more order than those minsters provided, and particularly the introduction of monks following a revised form of the Rule of St Benedict in churches that had for long been occupied by clergy living a less regulated and more relaxed way of life. Glastonbury, thanks to Dunstan, was thus reformed along the lines already adopted on the continent, and Muchelney probably followed its example. Over the next century or so some of the other ancient, minster-based communities seem to have closed or been absorbed: East Pennard was acquired by Glastonbury, Pitminster by Winchester, Banwell, Cheddar and eventually Carhampton went to increase the income of the bishops of Wells, Bedminster to endow Salisbury cathedral. The future lay with powerful bishops and influential cathedrals, but Frome and Milborne Port, with much less justification, had by the 1070s come into the hands of a politician.

BISHOPS AND THE NATION

Athelm was translated to Canterbury after fifteen or so years at Wells, and so was his immediate successor, Wulfhelm I; presumably both men were thought by kings Edward the Elder and Athelstan to be suitable men to be leaders of the national church. Our fifth bishop, Byrhthelm, was also promoted to Canterbury but was there for only a short time and returned to Wells. After him came a succession of men, all of them Saxons with what seem almost unpronounceable names and all monks, formerly heads of monasteries outside the diocese: Cyneweard, Sigegar, Aelfwine, Lyfing (or Aethelstan), Aethelwine, Brihtwine and Brihtwig (or Merehwit). Lyfing had been abbot of Chertsey and was translated to Canterbury in the emergency after the murder of Archbishop Aelfheah (Alphege) by the Danes at Greenwich. None of those men, curiously, seem to have been concerned to introduce monks to their cathedral.

There is no reason to suppose that those bishops were not active men. They figure, as would be expected, as members of the national assembly known as the Witan, the beginning of the long

Holcombe Old Church. Robert Dunning

Below: *Holcombe Old Church: inscription (inverted) recording its consecration in 928.* Robert Dunning

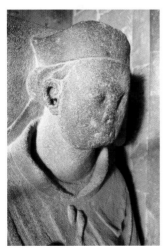

Duduc, bishop 1033-61: monument in Wells cathedral. Richard Neale

process that brought them later to membership of the House of Lords; and they witnessed royal documents as successive kings moved from place to place. Wulfhelm I as well as Archbishop Athelm put their names to a grant of land in the isle of Thanet to St Augustine's, Canterbury, in 925, Aelfheah was at meetings of the Witan at Exeter in 928, at 'Lullyngmynstre' in 930, and at Colchester, Worthy (Hampshire) and Luton in 931. Incidentally, also present at Exeter in 928 was Wrotard, archbishop of York, the very same man whose name on an inscription at Holcombe old church shows that he must have consecrated it on his way there or back, presumably with the full knowledge and approval of Bishop Aelfheah.

After a succession of twelve native bishops came the first of men with continental origins, men quite different from the Saxon monks of the tenth century. The first was Duduc, either from Lotharingia or Saxony, a man very close to King Cnut who appointed him in 1033. Like his predecessors he witnessed royal charters such as the gift of Littleham (Devon) to Ordgar in 1042 or the endowment of Stow (Lincolnshire) in 1053-5. More significant was his appointment by Edward the Confessor to attend the synod of Rheims in 1049. Duduc died in 1061 and was succeeded by another foreigner, Giso, Edward's own chaplain and a native of St Trond near Liege but usually known as Giso of Lorraine. Giso was consecrated bishop in Rome by Pope Nicholas II.

PASTORS OF THE FLOCK

So those bishops of Wells along with their fellows played a full part in the affairs of state but they were none of them, so far as we know, reformers in the mould of Dunstan. Laws issued by King Athelstan in the 930s required that 'all servants of God' at every minster were to sing 50 psalms for the king each Friday, and those of King Edmund in the 940s hint that standards needed to be improved when they declared that priests ought to be celibate as examples of purity of life, that church taxes (tithes, church scot, Rome money and plough alms) were paid reluctantly and that church buildings needed attention - every bishop was to put the churches on his own estates in repair and the king was encouraged by his counsellors to require that secular lords should act similarly 'as we have great need'.

Laws of the 960s in the time of King Edgar (crowned at Bath in 973 in a service which emphasised his priestly role and was the model for later ceremonies) envisaged a countryside that still had old minsters to which some parishes belonged, but also churches built by landowners with graveyards on sites leased from the crown, to which a third of each man's tithe was to be given There were also churches without graveyards. King Edgar declared each Sunday to be a festival that was to last from Saturday noon to dawn on Monday. The weekend was born.

In the 990s Aelfric Grammaticus or Aelfric the Homilist, a monk much influenced by Bishop Aethelwold of Winchester, one of Dunstan's fellow reformers, wrote a pastoral letter to his own bishop outlining the work of everyone in minor or holy orders, that is all who served the churches of the land. His standards were undoubtedly high. He recommended that all churches should have seven services every day and that every priest should have at least ten books in order to carry out his ministry, namely three parts of the Bible (the psalter, the epistles and the gospels), prayers and song books, and lives of saints. Such a small library equipped the priest to consecrate the eucharist and teach the faith, placing him at the top of a hierarchy that began at the bottom with the ostiarius, the door keeper, rather like a sexton who was to guard the church, locking believers in and unbelievers out; then the lector who read God's word, then the exorcist who adjured accursed spirits and later read over the insane and infirm. The acolyte carried candle or taper when the gospel was read and the eucharist consecrated; the subdeacon served the deacon with the sacred vessels at mass; the deacon set the offerings, read the gospel, and might baptise and give communion. And outside the church services priests attended synods where they reported any kind of opposition including difficult parishioners and were encouraged to prepare the young for service. The church regulations of King Edgar suggest that some priests were quarrelling among themselves (referring the matter to the bishop only 'if one needs must'), were evidently taking one another's scholars, were sometimes refusing to offer baptism and confession, and were leaving young people too long unconfirmed. The teaching role of the clergy, so Aelfric Grammaticus declared, involved telling people the meaning of the gospel in English at celebrations of the eucharist and also the lord's prayer and the creed, though not all priests, it was admitted, could understand Latin. Aelfric also reminded priests that they should not move from church to church, that tithes were to be given for church repairs, for the poor, and for 'God's servants who look after the church' in equal portions, and that bread for the eucharist should not be kept too long lest it go mouldy or be eaten by mice.

The bishops had oversight (*episcopus* means overseer) for, as Archbishop Aelfric of York wrote, 'greater benediction'. He confirmed the young, consecrated churches and churchyards, ordained priests, blessed the oils. Yet the bishop's position among the leaders of the nation just possibly encouraged him to forget to be humble. More than one writer suggested that bishops were rather showy in their dress and charged large fees, and Archbishop Wulfstan of York in the early eleventh century seems to imply that not all preached God's law and forbade wrong but were 'afraid and ... ashamed of the right, and mumble[d] with their jaws when they ought to cry aloud'. The model bishop supported his fellows, chose excellent counsellors, especially in priest's orders, who accompanied him on his travels around his diocese to offer advice and act as witnesses to his decisions, and presided over his priests in synod equipped to refer any of its business to the general regulations of the church. The personal qualities of the early bishops of Wells are quite unknown, but Duduc clearly understood the importance of sensible financial support. When he came he found just four canons at Wells and very little money to support himself and them, but somehow he had already acquired the monastery of St Peter at Gloucester and the old minsters at Banwell and Congresbury. On his death, however, they were taken by the powerful Earl Harold and the dreadful Archbishop Stigand. Perhaps that was one reason why Duduc's successor-but-one, John of Tours, took himself off to the relative comfort of Bath.

Giso, bishop from 1060 to 1088, came from Lorraine, perhaps bringing with him some of the reforming ideas then influencing the continent. Those ideas included more efficient methods of government, and at Wells Bishop Giso had the support of an archdeacon and several clergy called canons (because they lived by a Rule) and by a provost who served as the steward of the estates that supported them. About 1090 Giso's successor, John of Tours, for all sorts of complicated reasons that were in part political, decided to settle in Bath. He thus removed his seat from Wells to the abbey church at Bath, pulled down the refectory, cloister and dormitory where the Wells canons had eaten, studied and slept, and left them to fend for themselves. Their income was put into the not too generous care of a new provost, who just happened to be Bishop John's brother. The centre of the Somerset see moved to its edge, with imaginable consequences.

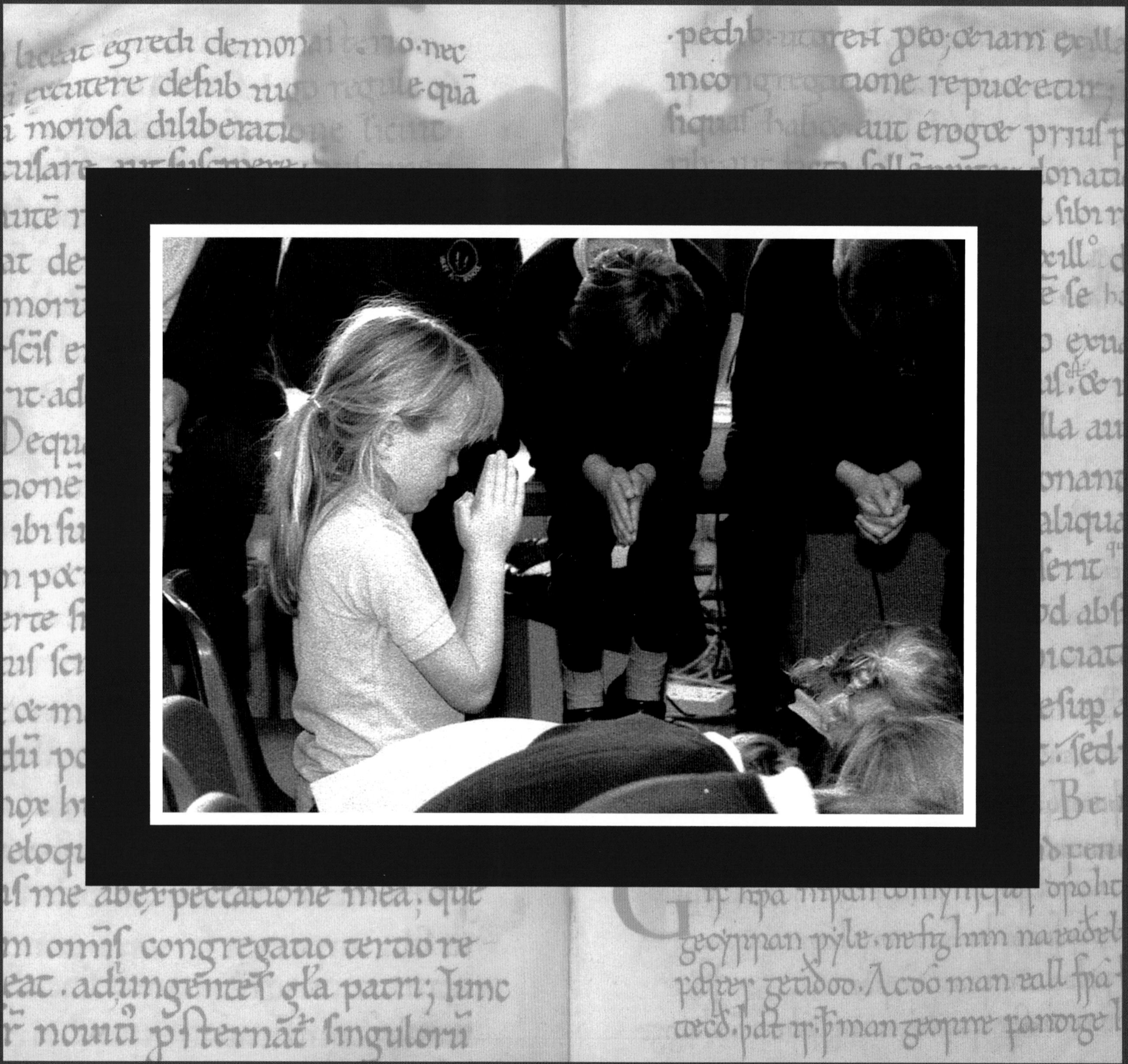

2
Pray Constantly

I Thessalonians 5.17

'Seven times in the day I have rendered praise to You' and 'In the middle of the night I rose to glorify You'. For St Benedict, writing in Italy at the beginning of the sixth century, the words of the Psalmist were the inspiration for the 'Work of God' (*Opus Dei*), the daily and nightly acts of worship that gave those who lived by his Rule a special aim and purpose. Masses, processions and the commemoration of saints were gradually added to that round of recitation of the psalms and canticles, and were accompanied by more or less elaborate rituals, musical accompaniments, vestments and special furnishings in both cathedral and monastic churches. Together they offered to those who took part and to those who listened from afar a moving

The Rule of St Benedict, damaged by being held too near a guttering candle. (© Dean and Chapter of Wells)

Opposite page: *Pray constantly.* Phil Day 2004 (© Templar Trust)

17

West front, Wells cathedral.
Richard Neale

spiritual experience and a taste of Heaven. Yet those who were part of the experience were also human. St Benedict had recognised that while many of the Fathers of the Church had made a practice of reciting all the psalms each day, there would be those who, try as they might, could not hope to do the same. He thus arranged that even the laziest monk would at least manage to say them all during the course of a week. That, too, was to prove for many a difficult challenge and perhaps the greatest criticism of monastic life in England in the early sixteenth century. After the dissolution of the monasteries in the diocese, the canons of Wells and their vicars choral alone in Somerset continued a daily round of worship until monks returned to England in the eighteenth century.

❈ ❈ ❈

When King Edward the Elder divided the great see of Sherborne in 909 he brought Athelm out of the monastery of Glastonbury and gave him the minster at Wells as the centre of his new work in Somerset. The difference between monastery and minster (both words deriving from the Latin *monasterium*, itself coming from a Greek word meaning to live alone) would soon become apparent as the result of reforms which were introduced by St Dunstan some thirty years later, but until then both monastery and minster aspired to be places of prayer and learning where communities of clergy worshipped together, taught all who would listen and then spread the gospel. Glastonbury at that time was outstanding: it produced at least seven of the first twelve bishops of Wells and bishops for seven other sees, notably Dunstan himself who went via Worcester and London to Canterbury where he led the church in England from 959 until his death in 988. Bath, of the other Somerset Christian communities, also produced an archbishop of Canterbury in the person of the martyr-saint Alphege, murdered by Vikings in 1012.

Great damage had obviously been done to both minsters and monasteries by the Vikings in their raids in the ninth century and King Alfred's purpose in founding Athelney as a community of monks was to restore a life of quiet study in his kingdom. So damaged was Wessex, indeed, that he had to draw members of the new community from abroad and they soon discovered that living together was not easy. Alfred's own personal efforts in translating into English an essential guide to pastoral care proved crucial in the restoration of the kingdom, the reconstruction of both minsters and monasteries, and the development of the English language, that last a claim which was later to be made for the Authorized Version of the Bible.

The movement for the reform of religious communities originating on the continent inspired Dunstan while in exile there. With Aethelwold, another former monk from Glastonbury and bishop of Winchester 963-84, and Oswald, bishop of Worcester 961-92 and archbishop of York 971-92, they together transformed many of the established monasteries and raised their standards. Bath and Glastonbury were certainly improved and their members focussed on a common life with prayer and study at its centre. Those unwilling to accept the regular and regulated life demanded were removed, perhaps going to join those clerks for whom the less strict life in a minster was more acceptable.

Many of those minsters at least retained some of their original ideals even though by the time of the Norman Conquest they had lost their communities and were instead rather rich parish churches whose estates were clearly attractive to potential owners. Northover was thus first swallowed up by Glastonbury abbey but by 1086 had come into the hands of the greedy Maurice, bishop of London, Banwell became part of the endowment of the bishops of Wells, Frome and Milborne Port were grabbed by Regenbald, a powerful member of Edward the Confessor's court. Bruton and Taunton, with the help of powerful patrons who may have taken some of their land, were allowed to transform themselves into houses of canons following the Rule of St Augustine of Hippo. Those who belonged to such houses came, rather nonsensically, to be called regular canons, both words meaning that they followed a Rule.

FROM MINSTER TO CATHEDRAL

The minster at Wells followed a different course. Since 909 it had been the cathedral of Somerset and in Bishop Giso's time its canons together shared a large part of Wells manor and some property at Litton and Wanstrow. After Bishop John of Tours had gone to Bath and turned them out of house and home their survival was something of a miracle. Robert of Lewes, bishop 1133-66, was a man who understood the importance of community life for he had been a member of the monastery of St Pancras at Lewes, one of the stricter kind of houses looking to Cluny in Burgundy as their inspiration. He came, though, not as a simple monk but as one who had been employed to put Glastonbury in order after the shambles left by Abbot Seffrid, and was the first English-born bishop in Somerset since the Conquest. Bishop Robert seems to have recognised that Wells would make a convenient place from which to administer his large diocese. He did not abandon his cathedral at Bath, but he early set about transforming King Ine's minster into something powerful and important.

He did it by giving it some of the property Bishop Giso had held and by drawing up a constitution under which it could be governed and its members regulated. The result of the first action was that by his death he had built up a community of over thirty men who had roles to play either in the minster or in the diocese and who each had an income from an estate, usually called a prebend (and hence the holder was a prebendary), from a Latin word from which provender also comes. Under Bishop Robert's successor, the Italian-born Reginald FitzJocelin, Bath still remained the cathedral, but more land was given or bought for Wells, thus allowing more prebendaries to be appointed; and at the same time a new church was started, close by the old minster, at the heart of which would be a special area for all those prebendaries to sit, sing and pray together. The next two bishops, Savaric and Jocelin, saw the number of prebends increased still further so that by 1242 when Jocelin died there were 52, the new building was completed and, within a year or two, the minster became a cathedral again.

The canons of Wells (a less clumsy way to describe them, but they are also sometimes called the dean and chapter or less formally the chapter) had much earlier been asserting themselves in the diocese. By virtue of their estates, either held collectively to provide a shared income called 'commons', or as individual prebendaries, they had become important landowners in Somerset and beyond holding, for instance, most of Combe St Nicholas, Wedmore and Winsham and they often challenged other landowners such as Glastonbury and Muchelney abbeys for rights on the rich grasslands of the moors in the heart of the diocese. In 1173 they successfully claimed the right to help the monks of Bath choose their next bishop, the real legacy of Bishop Robert. In 1206 46 canons of Wells and 40 monks of Bath together were involved in the choice of Bishop Jocelin of Wells, one of their fellow canons and a native. And while Jocelin was first known as bishop of Bath and Glastonbury and later simply bishop of Bath, he clearly saw Wells as his continuing home and around 1206 built what is still the core of the Bishop's Palace.

At his death in 1242 the monks of Bath, unwilling to share with the canons the choice of his successor, tried to get in first by applying to the king for a licence to proceed, but on appeal the pope ruled not only that the canons of Wells should have an equal say in the matter, but that the next bishop and his successors should set up their seat in both churches. Roger of Salisbury, the next bishop, was from 1245 the first bishop of Bath and Wells.

❈ ❈ ❈

When William Cosyn became dean of Wells in 1498 he was no stranger to the cathedral, where he was already archdeacon of Bath and prebendary of Ilton, and where his uncle, Oliver King, was bishop. He thus understood the intricacies of the election process that had brought him to office, and one of his earliest actions was to compile a book of legal precedents from which he might find guidance as to what he could and could not do now that he was dean. That book includes a detailed description of the way in which the by then highly complicated rituals of worship were carried out. So much depended on local precedent, more on the demands of various festivals introduced into the Church's calendar since the time of Bishop Robert. But prayer was still at the heart of the cathedral.

Superficial reading of the rules that Dean Cosyn copied out might suggest that there was too much about complicated rituals, but more than three centuries of experience since Bishop Robert's time had taught that order and dignity were achieved, and thus worship offered at its very best, when all who took part had a well-ordered and well-conducted role. Bishop Robert's constitution had, in fact, set out the priorities of his foundation: a dean to lead the community, rather by the force of his personality as by his precise legal powers, as many deans found to their cost; and first after the dean a precentor, for his role in leading worship and supervising singers was of paramount importance. After the precentor (and precedence was sometimes bitterly fought over) came a chancellor, concerned with teaching and learning, the man who, embracing the bishop's teaching duties in his cathedral, was to organise schools of formation for adults and children. The chancellor was also the cathedral's chief archivist: the names of Thomas of Retford and Thomas Spert appear in one of its earliest record books. After the chancellor came the treasurer under whose care were the vestments and ornaments - copes, candles, crosses and the many other symbols of faith and samples of beauty that came to be deemed necessary and helpful in worship. Those four and Bishop Robert's right-hand man the archdeacon of Wells became the Famous Five, the *Quinque Personae* (Five Persons) by whom, with the necessary help of deputies such as a sub-dean and a succentor, the corporate life of the college-cathedral was regulated and continuous regular worship achieved as they and the other prebendaries occupied the stalls assigned to them in the quire to take part in the liturgy and to sit in proper order in the chapter house to deliberate and decide on the business of the day.

Within a very short time, of course, there were modifications to the constitution. If Bishop

Vicars' Close, Wells.
Robert Dunning

Robert had envisaged that all his prebendaries would carry out their duties in person he would have been disappointed. Some of them very soon found other more attractive posts and deputies known as vicars choral came to take their places at regular services. By the 1240s those vicars were seen as an almost corporate body, subject to common rules of behaviour and to measures to improve their performance, for on the whole they were not the most distinguished and devout people but rather junior clergy hoping for promotion but never with a guarantee of achieving it. Their picturesque college, eventually provided for them by Bishop Ralph of Shrewsbury in the months before the Black Death struck, was an attempt to bring them together and provide them with a respectable and more dignified way of life than had before been possible. Some of the houses in the Vicars Close are still occupied by men who are professionally involved in the musical life of the cathedral.

Singing boys, choristers, were from the beginning also part of the cathedral's cycle of prayer. There were only six of them in Bishop Robert's time and they sat on the lowest benches, with other boys perhaps destined for the priesthood beside and behind them. They were chosen by the precentor, who was responsible for their education as both readers and singers. They, like the vicars choral, were given a place to live together by Bishop Ralph of Shrewsbury; and visitors to the cathedral's new refectory may imagine themselves in his Song School, the remains of which are around them. There, under new rules drawn up by Bishop Bekynton in the mid 15th century, they were under the care of a master who chose and trained them for the choir duties under the direction of the precentor, taught them good table manners - not to drink with mouths full, not to gnaw their bread, not to dirty their table cloth nor to pick their teeth with their knives - and after games around supper time sent them to sleep three in a bed, two smaller ones with their heads at the top of the bed, the older one with his head at the foot.

How some things change and some things stay the same! About 1323 Bishop Droxford agreed with the decision of the chapter that canons could, in spite of tradition, bring books and their own lights into the quire; but the vicars choral had to continue to learn the words 'lest they should become more negligent than ever'. A would-be chorister towards the end of the First World War presented himself at the home of Dr Thomas Davis, remarkably both precentor and organist, and was required to sing a hymn. Luckily the boy knew it and was accepted at once provided he had his tonsils and adenoids removed. A scholarship gave him education at the cathedral school but did not shield him from caning if he sang a wrong note and fines of up to 2s 6d (12p), collected monthly. The rewards for at least one chorister were the joy of singing and Sunday evenings at the Deanery with Mrs Armitage Robinson.

In 1377, when the government in financial difficulties decided to levy a tax not on goods and property but on heads, counted nearly 90 men living close to the cathedral and employed in its mission: Dean Stephen Pempel and 16 prebendaries including the precentor, the chancellor, the sub-dean and the succentor, and 38 vicars choral. Among those lesser folk were altarists, who sat in the second row behind the choristers and served the priests who sang masses in the many chantries. And among them, too, were three men called *tabulatores* who acted as prefects, appointed by the chancellor but assigned to their duties by the succentor, who ensured that singing, serving and reading at the services were carried out with proper dignity and competence. As they shared the fines imposed for failure, they were no doubt very keen to report faults.

And faults there must have been, for the services at the cathedral by the later fifteenth century were immensely complicated and required a detailed book of rules indicating who should take part, where they should stand and what they should wear. Rehearsals must have been endless. When to stand, when to sit, when to move and in what order must have left young choristers if not others bewildered and on edge. Those rules leave the reader in no doubt that there was a simple purpose behind the apparent unnecessary detail. Even the most senior member needed to be reminded to bow to the altar when crossing the quire from one side to the other and there was to be no undue haste: 'on entering and leaving their places they must go quietly and not jump over the forms'. This was a place of prayer, the House of God, the gate of heaven.

The Chain Gate, the bridge from the vicars' houses to the cathedral.
Robert Dunning

SECULAR COLLEGES

The cathedral without a bishop was first a minster and later in strictly legal doctrine a secular college, a group of priests living in some sort of loose community whose purpose was principally to worship God. It spawned long after it returned to cathedral status two smaller colleges: the first when Bishop Ralph of Shrewsbury brought the vicars choral together in 1348 with houses and a common hall, to which were added the present chapel in the 1420s, a treasury in the 1430s and the Chain Gate in 1459-60 which sheltered the vicars from the elements when they passed to and from the cathedral. Almost from the first the vicars choral had their own chaplain who said mass daily somewhere in the new buildings and later in their chapel at the north end of the college. In gratitude for the bridge they undertook in 1460 to say the Lord's Prayer and Hail Mary every time they crossed it for the soul of their founder and the benefit of their current patron, and to say psalms and prayers at Ralph of Shrewsbury's tomb and beside the chapel Bekynton had already prepared to house his tomb. A second college was created when Bishop Erghum about 1399 eventually provided a permanent building to house the cathedral's chantry and anniversary chaplains, some of whom had been living together since the 1330s.

There were other similar but much smaller colleges elsewhere in the diocese, the earliest founded at Stoke Sub Hamdon by Sir John Beauchamp in 1304. Four priests under a provost were employed at the now-vanished St Nicholas's chapel in the main village and housed in what is still called the Priory. In the chapel they were to sing five daily masses and other services for the founder's family, for the king, the bishop, and all faithful people, a demand that evidently proved

The order of the procession on Ascension Day before mass, to be sung by three clerks of the higher grade in silk copes 1501.

The south transept of Puckington church, built to make space for the extra priests of the little college. Robert Dunning

The chancel of North Cadbury church, its window sills high to allow for stalls. Hugh and Bridget Playfair

too great. By the early sixteenth century a single chaplain said mass three times a week.

Two other foundations in some sense hardly merit the name college. One was at the unlikely church of Puckington where an archpriest (implying a group of priests) was mentioned between 1312 and 1362. At Kilve a 'minister' and four priests were living together at what is still called Kilve Priory north of the parish church by 1332. That foundation, a rather grand chantry for the Furneaux family, probably did not outlast the century. The last Somerset college, by then almost an anachronism, was begun by Lady Elizabeth Botreaux at North Cadbury in 1417 and was to have six chaplains under a rector and four clerks. They were to pray for the king, for the founder and her son, for the souls of benefactors and friends and especially for her late husband and his parents. The foundress rebuilt the parish church, where the high sills of the chancel windows show that stalls for the rector and clerks were built or at least planned. In 1548 it was still called a college, staffed by a rector and two chaplains. What might have been a fourth college, that of St Martin at Milverton, had an even more fragile existence. A clerk employed to copy out the names and particulars of men ordained in Bishop Stillington's time had a serious lapse of concentration when he came to record that Master John Wyppill was made a subdeacon on 9 March 1476. He described him as a fellow of the college when he should have written that he was a fellow of Merton college, Oxford. How he came to add Milverton is a mystery.

THE MONASTIC WAY

Just as in the cathedral the 'Work of God' was the centre of community life, affecting both its work and the shape of the building in which it was performed, so it was in the monastic church where the night stair leading directly from the dormitory to the church is a graphic reminder of the call of the night office. It was that offering of prayer and worship which inspired the royal founders of Glastonbury, Muchelney and Athelney and was to encourage the founders of the other religious houses in the diocese. Founders and patrons wanted to enjoy the spiritual benefits of effective praying communities where they might at the end of their lives become lay members and thereafter be buried, as well as enjoying the cultural fame or social action of a lively house to their neighbourhood.

Each founder, of course, had a favourite 'family' of monks: William of Mortain looked to the reforming abbey at Cluny to inspire his new priory at Montacute at the end of the eleventh century, William de Roumare, founder of the abbey at Cleeve at the end of the 12th, followed in the steps of his grandfather, who had founded the Cistercian house at Revesby in his native Lincolnshire and chose the remote 'flowery valley' in the Brendons to established a pioneer-farming community in the tradition of the great Cistercian abbeys of the North of England. William de Mohun of Dunster is regarded as the founder of the priory (later abbey) at Bruton about 1142, probably successor to the minster there and a member of the Augustinians, the religious order named after St Augustine of Hippo.

Bishops were also founders in Somerset, though one, Robert of Lewes, a distinguished Cluniac monk, is known to have opposed the appearance of a rival Cistercian house in his diocese. William Giffard, bishop of Winchester and thus lord of Taunton, gave the community of the old minster beside his castle a new site outside the town about 1115 and was regarded as its founder; Bishop Reginald of Bath set up a hospital at Bath in 1180 and the Wells brothers, Hugh and Jocelin, respectively bishops of Lincoln and Bath, saw the hospital of Wells established at the beginning of the thirteenth century. One of the last royal monastic foundations was on a miserable site in Selwood forest at Witham where a group of Carthusian monks from Burgundy were induced to settle in order to make good the promise of Henry II to found religious houses in expiation of his responsibility for the murder of Archbishop Becket.

Those houses, and others for men at Barlinch and Dunster in the far west, Stogursey (where French monks settled from Lonlay in Normandy), Woodspring, Keynsham and Hinton, and for women at Cannington and Barrow Gurney in their different ways and often as much smaller communities, took up the challenge to be places of prayer. Other hospitals at Bedminster, Bath and Bridgwater concentrated on service, and houses of friars at Ilchester and Bridgwater on preaching. Together they offered their prayers and practical support for the work of successive bishops, the friars, for instance, often acting as confessors and peripatetic teachers, the nuns supplying refuges and finishing schools for girls, the hospitals an immense amount of care for the poor and sick.

All religious houses were landowners with tenants to be concerned with, labourers to employ; they were often owners of churches with responsibility for appointing parish priests, maintaining chancels, paying chaplains. Glastonbury, the richest house in the land at the time of Domesday and second only to Westminster at the time of the Dissolution, owned much of central Somerset and at times clearly rivalled the bishops of the diocese in power and influence: united in prayer but sometimes divided by possessions. Yet the concern of successive bishops for the standards to be achieved at the religious communities of the diocese are witness to the value they placed on the role of men and women who devoted their lives to their communities.

A moment of relaxation and humour, Cleeve abbey. Robert Dunning

Those who entered the religious life were, as St Benedict anticipated, men and women like any other; those who are to be found in the historic record are often the aggressive or the inadequate, and it must be admitted that the hopes of parents to have a son or daughter as a monk or nun may have been as much social aspiration as a sacrifice and may not have produced a person of profound prayer and deep piety. It was, frankly, difficult to pray when the pangs of hunger became unbearable. Isabella Poleyns and Joan Bozum, sisters at the poor nunnery at Barrow Gurney, suffered so much that at the end of the fourteenth century they left their house without the permission of their prioress and went over to the nunnery at Usk in Wales. They found to their dismay that food was no more plentiful there and begged to return; they still valued the life they had chosen, whatever the cost.

There were in Somerset some outstanding monks and nuns, but their quiet and devout lives have left no record. A few others were remarkable. The Carthusians were specialists in holiness, for theirs was a life of contemplation, each largely confined to a tiny cell. St Hugh of Avalon, later bishop of Lincoln, was the first prior to stay long enough at Witham to make an impression, and the community he created attracted Adam, a learned and pious Scot from Dryburgh, Prior Walter from Bath and Prior Robert from St Swithun's, Winchester. Adam of Dryburgh's various works - 'Soliquy on the Instruction of the Soul', 'On the Fourfold Discipline of the Cell', 'The Mirror of Discipline' and 'My Own Secret'- were widely read and clear evidence of the depth of his intellect and piety.

Those remarkable men were at Witham in its early years at the end of the twelfth century. In the 15th, when all about them were apparently losing their way, the piety of the Carthusians attracted the attention of Henry V who gave Witham some land to ease their financial burdens, and Edward IV who gave both Witham and Hinton an annual grant of wine from Bristol 'for the sustenance of their bodies, weakened by their vigils and fasts'. John Luscote from Hinton and John Blacman of Witham were among the intellectuals of the later Middle Ages, and at the Dissolution both houses had no room for recruits. For years both featured in the wills of the devout who requested the prayers of the brothers, and in Edmund Horde, the last prior of Hinton, was a man very tempted to defy the King's Visitors in 1539 when they came to close it.

By contrast the intellect and piety of generations of monks of Glastonbury had turned to the study of history, and their own in particular. That history was creatively modified in pursuance of the political battle with the bishop of the diocese but also to pay for a new church fit to be a major pilgrimage site, for the relics at Glastonbury were second to none and popes had offered many inducements to the faithful to pray at the holy site. That its main attractions were the tombs of three Saxon kings and King Arthur certainly distinguished it from the saintly burial places like Canterbury, Westminster or St David's, but made it hardly less popular with the pious pilgrim; and when Joseph of Arimathea was added to what may have been a flagging attraction, success was almost guaranteed. The abbey's ample income might well appeal to a certain type of recruit, but that is no explanation of the remarkable fact that men were almost flocking to join the community in the years of religious uncertainty in the 1530s when almost everywhere else the life of the cloister was fast losing its focus.

The initials of Abbot Bere at Westonzoyland, under whom Glastonbury abbey took on a new lease of life. Robert Dunning

PRIVATE PRAYER AND PERSONAL PIETY

Outside the cathedral, the smaller colleges and the monastic houses devotion and piety were to be found in varying measure. There were, for instance, individuals who deliberately shut themselves away from the world as hermits, most of them nameless but obviously of more than simply local notoriety. Among the earliest was the hermit of Crewkerne, who was given alms by Henry II in 1176–7. There were recluses living beside the chapel of St Thomas on Polden, in Edington parish, in 1241 and 1505, and in the fourteenth century there were several: Brother Thomas, formerly a monk from Muchelney was one of two who lived at Oath in Aller in 1328 who, having been enclosed, asked Bishop Droxford for leave to make a door to admit their confessor. In Bishop Ralph of Shrewsbury's time Philip Schipham went to live at a place called *Sancti Romani*, John de Worm of Glastonbury was permitted to lead the life of a hermit and Sybil of Forde moved into a specially-built chamber attached to Twerton church. In 1403 Robert Chard exchanged his cell at Forde abbey for something similar in Crewkerne churchyard and in the 1440s another nameless hermit was living at a chapel in South Cadbury, the remains of which stand beside the busy A 303 at Chapel Cross.

The most famous of all Somerset's hermits must be Wulfric of Haselbury who, to the amazement of his patron, turned his back on a promising career as parish priest of Compton Martin in favour of a tiny cell built against the parish church at Haselbury Plucknett. From there he dispensed holy wisdom to kings and peasants alike until his death in 1154 and then attracted pilgrims to his tomb, resulting in the claim by the Cluniac monks of Montacute that his remains should be removed to their house, claims made the more urgent but ultimately unsuccessful because of reported miracles. One other local hermit may well have prayed and dispensed wisdom but also had a particular aim. He was Stephen Coye who in 1445 with Bishop Bekynton's approval was permitted to join the Rule of St Paul the Hermit and to collect money for road repairs between Bristol and Dundry.

More commonly, private devotion on the part of people of means was expressed in the chapels and oratories they formed in their houses, often very small spaces where the family might gather for private prayers or where a priest might come to say mass. Private prayers might be found in a book like the one still surviving that almost certainly belonged to Margaret, born Margaret Coker, who married first Sir Alexander Hody and second Sir Reginald Stourton. Cokers had lived in a manor house at West Bower for generations and in 1339 Bishop Ralph of Shrewsbury had allowed Richard Coker to have mass said in his oratory there for a year. More than a century later, in 1462 when the widowed Margaret was planning to marry again, Bishop Bekynton granted her and her husband-to-be a special licence to be wed in their own chapel of St John the Baptist at Bower, provided only that the vicar of Bridgwater agreed and their banns were published.

Chapels and oratories like the one at Bower were to be found in large numbers throughout the diocese. Only when it was proposed to have mass said or sung was the bishop involved, for there was a danger that people might be drawn away from their parish church. Licences therefore were usually given for a short period and often for good reason, such as the ill health of the owner. In the 17 years from 1311 Bishop Droxford licensed 31 such chapels and from 1331 to 1353 Bishop Ralph

Former chapel and hermitage at Chapel Cross, South Cadbury.
Hugh and Bridget Playfair

Beginning of document by which John Kendall, a Bridgwater merchant, his wife and family are made secular members of the Franciscan convent in the town, 1479.
Somerset Record Office D/B/bw 109

Sir Thomas Tremayle's chapel at the right side of his house at Blackmoor, Cannington by A A Clarke, 1859. Somerset Local Studies Library

allowed almost 70. Among them were three granted in 1316, one at Rhode in North Petherton on the grounds of distance from the parish church and floods, one at Hestercombe because of distance and one at Rowdon in Stogumber for no apparent reason. Two among many such chapels survive in Cannington, one in a wing of Blackmoor Farm, the work of a lawyer, Sir Thomas Tremayle, at the end of the fifteenth century, the other at Gurney Manor, where a tiny chapel was squeezed into the west range in the early sixteenth century. Clearly, people with money wanted to pray.

And people with money wanted to secure salvation. One of the decisions taken under Pope Innocent III at the third Lateran Council in 1215 was embodied in a decree that stressed the importance of the mass. It put into words the mystery of the change from bread and wine to the body and blood of Christ that opened the way to immense possibilities. In a short time masses were being offered for individuals during their lives and for their souls after death. Very soon after his death in 1236 some land in Wells was given to the cathedral to pay for a service for the dead for ever for the souls of Bishop Jocelin, Dean Peter de Cestria, their predecessors and successors. By the end of the thirteenth century, similar endowments, commonly known as chantries, had been made to have masses said for Bishop William of Bitton I at the altar of St Mary, for Bishop William of Bitton II at the altar of Holy Cross, for John of Axbridge, once sub-dean, in the chapel of St Mary Magdalene, for John of Bitton, former provost, in the chapel of St Nicholas, for Walter of St Quinton, former archdeacon of Taunton, at the altar of the Holy Saviour, and for Canon Richard Bamfield in the chapel of St Edmund of Abingdon in the nave.

Official approval of the feast of Corpus Christi in 1264, which commemorated the gift of the Eucharist, brought wider awareness of such continuing prayer and chantries were founded in many parish churches and chapels. One of the earliest recorded in the diocese was founded by Agnes Monceaux, owner of half Crewkerne manor, in the Lady Chapel in Crewkerne churchyard in 1316. Not far away, at Limington, a chapel was built on the north side of the parish church where from 1329 a chantry priest celebrated mass daily for members for the family of Sir Richard de Gyverney. Sir Richard not only built the chapel but also provided for the priest a massbook, a chalice, vestments, and ornaments for the altar. The chaplain was to be permanently resident at his post, was to attend all services in the church, was at each Ascensiontide to concelebrate mass with the rector and offer bread to the poor, and was to hand over all offerings made in his chapel.

John Fichet, the first chaplain at Limington, and many another chantry priest, must have had time on their hands. Perhaps, if the rector did not do so, Fichet taught the children of the parish. That was certainly the case at Woolavington, where one of three chantry priests at the end of the fourteenth century kept a school at which one of his pupils was the son of the manorial hayward. Clearly a bright lad, John Hody went to Oxford, presumably under the patronage of his lord, Lord Audley, and held powerful positions in the dioceses of Bath and Wells and Worcester. At his death he wished to be buried in the same chapel where he had learnt his lessons.

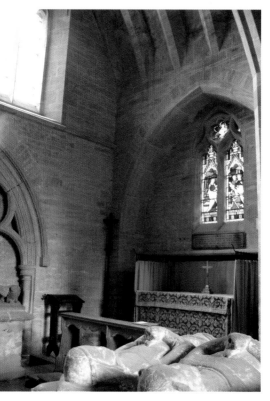

Limington church, the former chantry chapel founded in 1329.
Robert Dunning

One of the stories told about Glastonbury's past was of how the Norman abbot Thurstan attempted unsuccessfully to replace the traditional Gregorian plainsong by one from Fécamp that he evidently preferred. Monks were as sensitive to changes in musical style as modern congregations and Thurstan was met with united opposition. It was, perhaps, the catalyst in a growing quarrel that ended in violence and bloodshed and in Thurstan's removal to his native Caen in 1083. Herluin, his eventual successor and also from Caen, is remembered particularly for his rebuilding of the abbey church where, in the great choir, plainsong continued to be chanted.

Plainsong, variously described as subtle, majestic, austere and spiritual, was the method of singing originating in Rome and approved by Pope Gregory the Great. It was to be the glory of monastic worship, requiring much expertise for perfection and producing, at best, mind in harmony with voice in the sight of God and his Angels. Small houses, St Benedict had recognised, could hardly emulate the large in their antiphonal singing across a cavernous choir, but in a small and intimate space could still be a genuine expression of prayer and praise. Yet perfection may not regularly have been achieved. Archbishop Pecham when he formally visited Glastonbury in 1281 began his criticism with remarks on the quality of worship, and bishops of Bath and Wells in the fifteenth century almost always gave prominence to the need for improved liturgy. Bishop John Stafford in 1430 urged the canons of Bruton to be humble and devout at all times, and especially devout in rendering their services, avoiding unnecessary walking about during the singing of the offices or mass. Bishop Thomas Bekynton found the same sort of neglect there and at Keynsham, Muchelney and Athelney in the 1450s, revealing that at Muchelney poor copying of service books meant that the monks were not singing from the same hymn sheet and the result was discord. In spite of the criticism of Archbishop Pecham, Glastonbury had a better record: St Dunstan had given the abbey an organ, and a professional organist had been employed there at least since the beginning of the 14th century. And in 1534 Abbot Whiting appointed a 'singingman' in the same tradition: James Renynger was to sing and play the organ in the Lady Chapel at daily services and to sing and play for the choir monks in the abbey church at feasts and festivals, accompanying the choir monks as their voices crossed the great Choir from one side to the other in turn. But Renynger had other talents. Abbot Bere, Whiting's predecessor, had a harpist in his household; the new abbot wanted his musician to play and sing at Christmas parties and to teach boys how to play organs and sing 'in prick song and descant'.

In 1538, when the smaller monasteries had already been closed and a visitation was carried out at the king's order, there was some very frank speaking, not from the bishop but from the monks themselves. Young men from both Glastonbury and Athelney went so far as to say that services were tedious and involved 'much rendering of the psalms'. They clearly did not understand their essential purpose of continuous prayer and praise. They had the help at both houses of professional musicians, but Glastonbury, at least, had enough choir monks to sing in the traditional way. Sadly for those complaining young men the liturgy had lost its force and their religious life its purpose; that continuing cycle of prayer and praise that St Benedict had instituted was for them no longer important. Small wonder that when Glastonbury, Athelney and the rest were closed, there was little opposition.

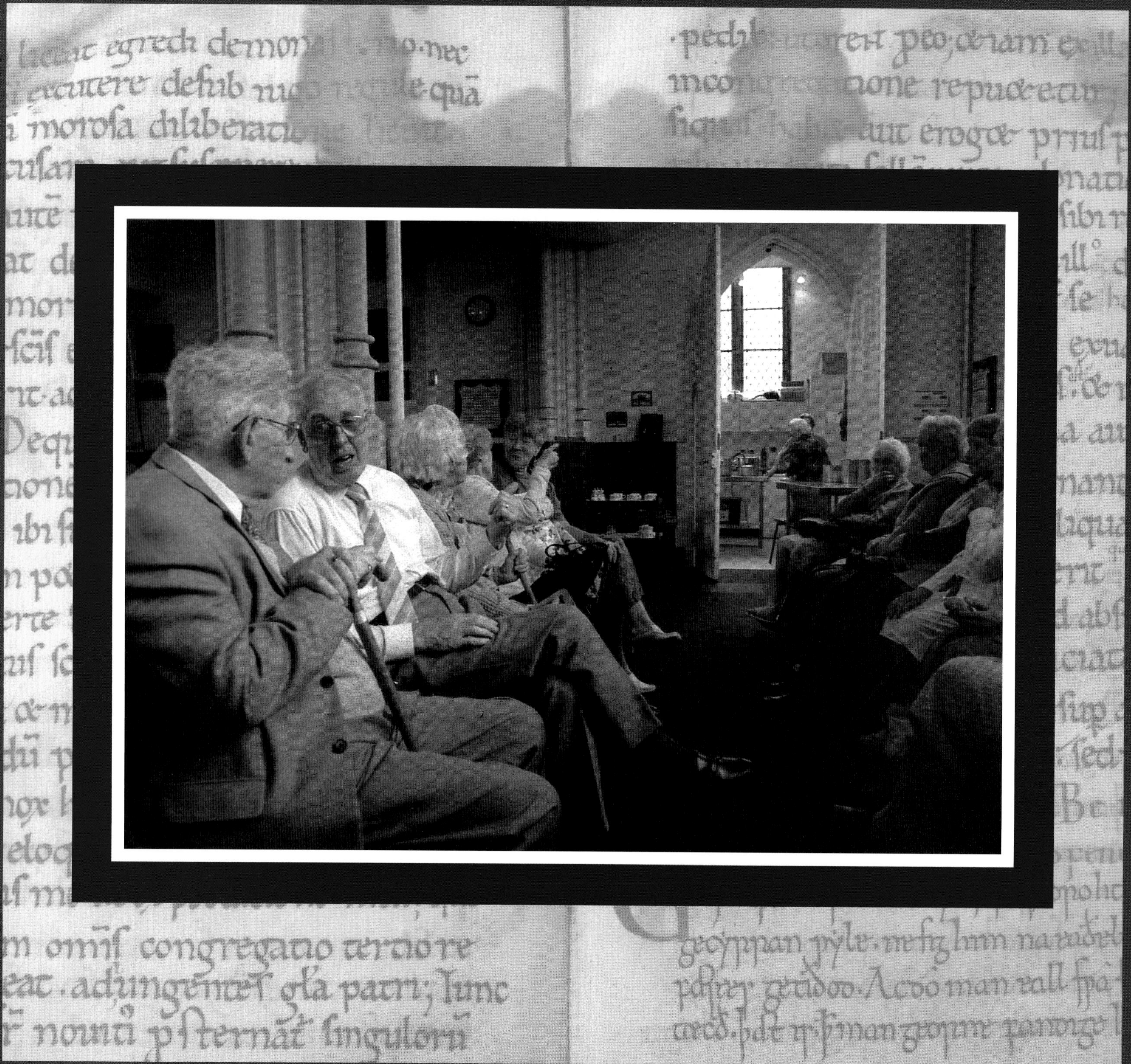

3

The Lord Raised up Judges

Judges 2.16

Against a background of political turmoil, warfare and plague in the Middle Ages, with human life so often held cheap, the church offered God's forgiveness for sin and hope for eternal life. The crucifix showing God identified with a world of grief and pain was a universal symbol; and the horror and hatred of any turning away from the faith and adopting some heresy was marked by a violent reaction in which compromise was impossible. Heresy must be rooted out by any means, however appalling, for the soul was at peril even if the body had been mistaken or misled.

And in an age of widespread illiteracy, the teaching of the faith had to be by recitation and rote as much as by explanation and example, by pictures in glass and paint, by the drama of the mass and processions, by structures in stone and wood that lifted the eyes and moved the spirit above the problems and pains of normal life. There was little question of changing communities; economics and social structures were underpinned by customs that kept the poor in their place and laws that by their nature were not progressive. Faith, as interpreted by the Fathers of the Church in its infancy, was a body of belief to be accepted without question for the health of the soul. The church was the embodiment of that faith on earth and its many structures and rituals were the means by which man entered heaven.

FATHERS IN GOD

Thomas Gascoigne, a learned theologian and for several years in the mid fifteenth century a canon of Wells was critical of the bishops of his time, saying they had been trained to combine the wisdom of the serpent with the innocence of the dove but that many had found the combination

Opposite page:
The Lord raised up Judges.
Phil Day 2004 (© Templar Trust)

33

so difficult to manage that they found it desirable to specialise. For five centuries until his own time most bishops had been either by training or experience lawyers or administrators, so their specialising was obvious. The bishops of Bath and Wells were no exception. Twenty-seven bishops between 1066 and 1500 were all in some way acceptable to the crown, some by personal service in the royal household, some as civil servants in royal administration. The bishopric was a reward for service done or to be done. The church thus provided their salaries, the crown the task; a bishopric was the result of a very satisfactory final salary pension plan and the income of the bishop of Bath and Wells was respectable enough for very senior civil servants.

Those men had long service records and their rewards had begun with single parishes, perhaps in the king's gift, a cathedral prebend where a bishop liked to put rising stars, and then an archdeaconry or a deanery. Several of our bishops already had knowledge of the diocese from their time as parish priests or prebendaries. Walter Haselshaw (1302-8) was the only one to have been dean of the cathedral but fourteen had been archdeacons here or elsewhere, and it was well known that archdeacons were very doubtful candidates for salvation.

Personal links with the king led some bishops into paths that took them far from their sees and on business that had nothing to do with saving souls. John of Tours (1088-1122) was described as 'familiar' of William Rufus and Godfrey (1123-35) was chaplain and chancellor to Henry I's queen, putting them both on the side of the crown against St Anselm in the great dispute with the papacy over bishops' appointments. Robert of Lewes (1136-66) was deeply involved on the side of King Stephen and his brother Henry of Blois in the civil war and wrote a chronicle recording

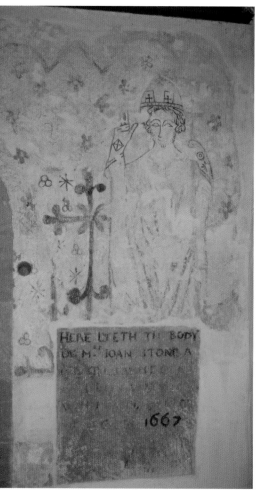

Judge or Pastor: my Lord Bishop offering his blessing at Sutton Bingham. Hugh and Bridget Playfair

The murder of Archbishop Becket, Marston Magna. Hugh and Bridget Playfair

the king's activities in the West of England. He was perhaps fortunate that age or illness kept him out of the great quarrel between Henry II and Archbishop Becket. However, two men with diocesan connections were deeply involved: Richard of Ilchester (probably born at Sock Dennis) and John Cumin (archdeacon of Bath c.1166-76) were Henry's ambassadors to the pope, and Reginald (1174-91) had in his youth served in the archbishop's household before joining his father, Bishop Jocelin de Bohun of Salisbury, on the other side. Reginald's successor Savaric (1191-1205) was related both to Reginald and to the Emperor Henry VI and played a leading role in negotiations for the release of Richard I from captivity.

John Harewell (bishop 1367-86). Richard Neale

The two Wells brothers, Hugh and Jocelin, were both clearly associated with the government of King John, and Jocelin (1206-42) retained his government post until after the Interdict had been published; he was probably the last bishop to go into exile at the end of 1209 when his brother Hugh was consecrated by Archbishop Langton. Robert Burnell, bishop 1275-92, died at Berwick on the king's campaign against the Scots (having, incidentally, also been elected both archbishop of Canterbury and bishop of Winchester).

John Harewell (1367-86) had been chaplain to the Black Prince, Ralph Erghum (1388-1400) a supporter of John of Gaunt, Henry Bowet (1401-7) a partisan of the claims of Gaunt's son Henry Bolingbroke who, as King Henry IV, appointed him. The two final political bishops were Robert Stillington (1466-91) and Richard Fox (1492-4), the first a close adherent of Edward IV but who found himself imprisoned in the Tower in 1478, under virtual house arrest in Oxford, and in prison again at Windsor castle in 1488-9, variously accused of involvement with the treason of the duke of Clarence and the rebellion of Perkin Warbeck. Richard Fox was by comparison a model of faithful service when he joined Henry Tudor in exile a year before his victory at Bosworth made him Henry VII.

The civil servants among the bishops from the 1260s were distinguished men, four of them - Walter Giffard (1264-6), Robert Burnell (1275-92), John Stafford (1425-43) and Robert Stillington (1466-91) - held the post of chancellor of England, the head of royal government, for much or all of the times they were bishops at Wells. But there were different ways of combining the two. Stafford regularly came to Somerset and was intimately concerned with the day-to-day business of the diocese; Stillington, so far as can be discovered, came down for just two months in 1476 during his 25-year rule, and that some time after he had ceased to be chancellor. Other people ran the diocese quite smoothly without him.

William Marchia (1293-1302) came as bishop after twelve years in government financial administration and John Droxford (1309-29) served in the royal treasury for even longer and was deeply involved in discovering who stole the crown jewels from Westminster in 1303. John Barnet (1364-6) was Treasurer of England all his time at Wells, Henry Bowet (1401-7) and Nicholas Bubwith (1407-24) for just a year. Bubwith had also served as keeper of Chancery Rolls, Thomas Bekynton, Robert Stillington and Richard Fox as keeper of the Privy Seal, an office of considerable

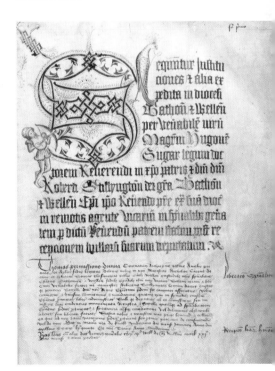

The opening page of Bishop Robert Stillington's register of official business. Somerset Record Office D/D/B reg 7

Above: *Former Treasury minister: John Droxford (bishop 1309-29).*
Richard Neale

Above centre: *Civil servant and humanist: Thomas Bekynton (bishop 1443-65): the tomb was made during the bishop's lifetime.*
Richard Neale

Above right: *Royal secretary and diplomat: Richard Fox, bishop of Bath and Wells 1492-4. Engraving of portrait when bishop of Winchester in 1516.*
Somerset Archaeological Society

intimacy with successive kings. Bekynton had also been Henry VI's secretary and deeply involved in international diplomacy. His appointment to Wells, much to the benefit of city and diocese, was oddly the reward of failure, for he had been unable to find the king an acceptable bride for the king among rival families in France. The girl who was eventually chosen, Margaret of Anjou, turned out to be a political disaster.

All those men, it goes without saying, were highly educated, usually lawyers: entirely suitable for their roles in royal government. There is no way of knowing whether beyond the conventional piety to be sensed in their official pronouncements and read in their wills they were deeply spiritual men with a passion for the faith they professed. They were men of their day, each holding an office whose demands had become formalised, its essentially pastoral role subsumed in a bureaucracy that had more to do with law than religion.

An absent bishop handed over his duties as judge and pastor to others so that the work of the diocese did not come to a standstill. Only a bishop could confirm children, consecrate chalices, churches and churchyards and ordain clergy, and when other duties called him away there were to be found bishops whose duties in Ireland or Wales were very light or whose people simply did not welcome them. Bishop Stephen, a Benedictine monk who was bishop of Waterford, dedicated the church at Combe St Nicholas at the request of Bishop Jocelin in 1239, and Bishop John Droxford was helped either by John Mac Cerbaill, bishop of Cork, Gilbert O'Tigernaig, bishop of Annaghdown, or John of Monmouth, bishop of Llandaff. In his early years at Wells Bishop Ralph of Shrewsbury received help from the bishop of Exeter and another bishop of Llandaff until, at the end of his life, he turned to the first of a succession of bishops whose exotic-sounding dioceses, mostly in the Middle East, they had no hope of reaching. These men were formally named suffragans, and were often monks, canons or friars. The first known in Somerset was John de Langbrugge, bishop of what is now Budva in Montenegro and then under Turkish rule. Later suffragans included the bishops of Holar in Iceland, of Selymbria and Christopolitanus near Istanbul and Sidon in Lebanon, as well as out-of-work Irish bishops of Innis Scattery and Ross. Probably the longest serving and most influential was Thomas Cornish, bishop of Tenos somewhere not far from Jerusalem, who was a member of the Order of St John. He was suffragan in Bath and Wells between 1485 and 1513 and in Exeter for most of that time, was provost of Oriel college in Oxford and successively chancellor and precentor in the cathedral. His fine tomb is at the foot of the chapter house steps.

The tomb of Thomas Cornish, bishop of Tenos, suffragan bishop 1485-1513. Michael Blandford (© Dean and Chapter of Wells)

A good many of the bishops of Bath and Wells were lawyers but still needed experts to deal with the day-to-day administration involving the niceties of church law. Bishop William of Bitton I in his 1258 'constitutions' referred to his 'official', his legal deputy, and when in 1325 Bishop Droxford appointed the bishop of Llandaff as a long-term deputy he made it clear he was to operate under the official's management, for he was to carry out the normal minor duties of a bishop such as 'reconciling' a churchyard polluted by bloodshed and to ordain candidates only after the official had examined them for suitability.

By the fifteenth century, when the habit of absentee bishops was well established, the administration of the diocese was in the hands of a small army of men, including lawyers for plaintiffs and defendants, registrars keeping records and apparitors (summoners) ensuring a steady flow of customers, and above them two judges, one called the official principal, the other the commissary-general, who ran the two main courts. And above even them, though actually sometimes the same men, were the bishop's chancellor (his legal adviser), and his vicar-general (an all-powerful diocesan secretary). Among the most influential in the fifteenth century were Dr Hugh Sugar, chancellor to Bishop Bekynton and official principal and vicar-general to Bishops Bekynton and

Stillington, whose charming chantry chapel in the cathedral is decorated with doctors' caps and sugar loaves; and Master Thomas Harris, a local lad from Long Sutton, who succeeded Sugar as treasurer of the cathedral, was the deputy of the archdeacon of Taunton, councillor to Henry VII, vicar-general to Bishop Stillington and was closely involved with the rebuilding of the chancel of North Curry church.

VENERABLE MEN

A bishop was charged with enormous responsibility, nothing less than the spiritual welfare of the clergy and people of his diocese – what other meaning could there be for his title 'Father in God'? Yet to be both judge of their misdeeds and pastor in their wanderings as well as a full-time royal servant was clearly impossible. Even to discover those misdeeds and wanderings required help, and the definition of misdeeds was a matter of dispute between church and state.

The bishop's direct concern, as Anglo-Saxon reformers had made clear, was with his clergy – their education and the quality of their pastoral care. The division of the diocese into rural deaneries was probably ancient and often coincided, as at Crewkerne, Ilminster and Taunton with one or more minster parishes; and it was 'immemorial custom' that the parish clergy of Bedminster and Bath deaneries, and no doubt in the other deaneries too, chose a rural dean each year. When archdeacons emerged rural deans took a step down and found themselves stooges of archdeacons as well as bishops, blamed together for taking heavy fees. Bishop William of Bitton I in 1258 tried to make them responsible to the bishop, a struggle that seems to have been won because archdeacons lost interest. So deans often found themselves acting for the bishop in local enquiries and their regular duty was to be the local agent for the bishop's court at Wells.

But the bishop needed more than a dozen or so clergy to help in his government of the diocese; a more permanent official than a rural dean was required, to be called an archdeacon, a title taken from the ancient church in Rome for a senior servant. The first in Somerset, in Bishop Giso's time, was Benselin, who was actually named in Domesday Book (1086). Several of his immediate successors served the bishop across the whole of the diocese; by 1106 there was so much business that three were needed, but not until the 1140s were they assigned to particular areas, one for Wells, one for Bath and a third, Hugh of Tournai, archdeacon 'beyond the Parrett'.

One of those three, the archdeacon of Wells, was evidently seen by Bishop Robert of Lewes as his deputy and was given a place of leadership in the college at Wells while he himself was based at Bath. The archdeacon of Wells is still one of only two archdeacons (the other is Canterbury) to be part of the cathedral's administrative body. In 1535 the then archdeacon had the prebend of Huish and Brent and the rectory of Berrow, with a total net income of over £144. The archdeacon of Taunton has from Bishop Jocelin's time held the prebend of Milverton I in the cathedral and in 1535 had over £83. The archdeacon of Bath did much less well, with no prebend attached to the post and in 1535 just the church of Stanton Drew and fees, giving a total of less than £26.

There was, in fact, a fourth archdeaconry though bishops did not care to admit the fact and instead usually referred to it as a jurisdiction, for it represented something of a failure. It was created almost by accident when Bishop Reginald thought he would like the abbot of Glastonbury to become a member of the chapter at Wells, thus in some way bringing him under the bishop's influence. Abbot Robert originally agreed, in return for an arrangement that ten churches in and around Glastonbury would remain under his exclusive care and that he and his successors would be archdeacons there. 'Frequent meetings and charges' that resulted from the arrangement persuaded him to change his mind and he resigned, thus losing Pilton and two other churches to Wells but he (or rather in time one of the senior monks in the community) retained responsibility for seven of the ten churches - St John's, Glastonbury, Street, Meare, Butleigh, Shapwick, Moorlinch and Sowy. Not long afterwards Bishop Jocelin, then titular head of the abbey, treated Thomas, archdeacon of Glastonbury, in exactly the way he treated his other archdeacons. Thomas's successors were all monks, appointed by the abbot and included Walter Oscote in 1392-3, Nicholas London in 1515, and John Phagan, in office at the Dissolution. As monks, those archdeacons had no personal possessions, but the account of Walter Oscote for his year of office shows a net income of less than £1.

Among the archdeacons of Wells, Taunton and Bath up to the sixteenth century were some very distinguished and some clearly absent men. John Cumin, one of Henry II's household clerks, somehow seized the archdeaconry of Bath with the king's support at the end of Bishop Robert's time and later became archbishop of Dublin. He was succeeded by Peter of Blois, the well-known writer of letters, sermons and theological works who had been chief secretary to Archbishop Richard of Dover, Becket's successor and friend of Bishop Reginald. He managed at the same time to be a canon of Rouen, Chartres, Bayeux and Salisbury cathedrals and also archdeacon of London. His contemporary, Thomas of Earley or Agnellus, archdeacon of Wells c1166-95, was also a writer of sermons.

Distinguished in other ways were Hugh of Wells (archdeacon of Wells 1204-6), brother of Bishop Jocelin, royal clerk, prebendary of London and Lincoln and between 1209 and 1235 bishop of Lincoln; John of Cheam, representative at the pope's court and briefly in 1259 archdeacon of Bath whom the pope made archbishop of Glasgow. Among the archdeacons of Taunton was William of Wrotham (c1204-17) who in 1207 found himself the rather unsuitable heir to the hereditary office of forester-in-fee for the whole of Somerset and that part of Exmoor in Devon.

Bishop Ralph of Shrewsbury had problems with all three archdeacons, beginning with Robert Hereward, archdeacon of Taunton, who had been appointed by Bishop Droxford just before Christmas 1320 and who had gone overseas to study liberal arts and law in the following summer.

How long he was away is not known but he had become used to the student life and had to promise Bishop Ralph not just to take orders from both bishop and other diocesan officers, but also to wear clothes and riding equipment proper to an archdeacon and also to promise to become a priest. All seems to have gone well for some years, apart from two court appearances for debt, but in 1340 Hereward was suspended from office for resisting the bishop's attempts to make administration more efficient. Three men claimed to be archdeacon of Wells between 1326 and 1332, one of them a candidate supported by the king and opposed by the bishop. So it was that in 1330, when Bishop Ralph as a matter of course ordered the archdeacon to induct the new rector of Rodney Stoke, his registrar noted that 'the lord having heard that no one exercised the office of archdeacon there, wrote to the rural dean of Axbridge to induct him if the truth of the matter agreed with public report'. Later in the same year the rural dean of Ilchester inducted the new priest at Charlton Mackrell. An archdeacon of Bath Matthew de Valenciis, appointed by the pope by August 1333 and only in deacon's orders, was not acceptable to Bishop Ralph and received a curious letter from the bishop's official telling him the bishop was prepared to allow him to continue to act until such time as 'the bishop shall think fit to do something else in that behalf'. Two years later the bishop successfully engineered his appointment as sub-dean at the cathedral in exchange with a man who was already a reliable member of his administrative staff.

Later in the Middle Ages the title and income of the archdeacon proved more attractive than the work. Three foreign cardinals followed each other as archdeacons of Wells between 1353 and 1369 and a fourth cardinal, Simon Langham, held office between 1369 and 1376, after his resignation as archbishop of Canterbury. Taunton, not to be outshone, was held by two foreign cardinals between 1373 and 1389, the second becoming Pope Boniface IX. Bath managed but one cardinal, in 1380.

In the fifteenth and the early sixteenth centuries Wells, obviously on account of its great wealth, attracted local men of distinction including the Renaissance scholar Andrew Holes (1450-70) and Dr Richard Nix (1494-1500), afterwards bishop of Norwich, and two foreigners, Dr Franceis de Basleiden (1500-2), who was archbishop of Besançon, and the amazing Italian Polydore Vergil (1508-54) who certainly lived at Wells for some of that time. The archdeacons of Bath of the time moved on to better-paid work, Dr Hugh Sugar to be the cathedral's treasurer after only three months in 1460 and William Cosyn, Bishop King's nephew, to be dean after a year in 1498. Four archdeacons of Taunton in the fifteenth century were promoted to bishoprics, another a few years after leaving, a tradition followed in the next half century by five more. (Incidentally, in the three centuries until 1857 one archdeacon of Taunton was made bishop (John White in 1554) and several internal moves were made from Bath to Taunton to Wells, obviously for financial reasons. But thereafter, until 1911, no Somerset archdeacon became a bishop until Charles Fane de Salis, archdeacon of Wells, was consecrated suffragan bishop of Taunton. History repeated itself in 2006 when Peter Maurice was similarly consecrated).

The 'Arms' of Dr Hugh Sugar on his chantry chapel, Wells cathedral: a doctor's cap and three sugar loaves. Richard Neale

SINS AND OMISSIONS

William the Conqueror gave bishops and archdeacons the right to deal with cases involving 'cure of souls' in their own courts and no longer in the traditional 'hundred' courts, but what sort of cases was a matter of argument. Marriage disputes and the administration of wills were clearly included but also contracts and therefore debt on the grounds that breach of faith was a moral question. And should not the church deal with all offending clergymen, whatever they had done? Archdeacons were clearly enthusiastic: Henry II reckoned they and rural deans between them made more money from fees and fines then he did from his own estates, and the archdeacon was popularly known as *oculus episcopi*, the bishop's eye or spymaster-general.

The same king, with the backing of most of his bishops (Bishop Robert was too ill to attend) at a meeting at the palace at Clarendon in 1164, drew up an agreement that allowed bishops and archdeacons to continue holding courts but made it clear, among many other things, that disputes over the right to present priests to parishes were a matter of state interest, that clergymen should appear at secular courts for secular offences, that the estates of bishops were held like the estates of laymen and that pleas of debt were a matter for the king's court.

The earliest example of a Somerset archdeacon in action is the record of a meeting of the Ilminster deanery chapter at Ashill about 1200 when Robert of Guildford, the archdeacon, reported the fact that Nicholas of Merriott had given to the canons of Bruton his chapel of Lopen. That was a legal matter and the archdeacon was clearly a legal officer. The building and the right to find a priest to serve it was passing from lay ownership to the church, an act that ensured that the canons of Bruton remained owners until 1539 when their house was dissolved. The formal document drawn up to mark the occasion was witnessed by Richard, the vice-archdeacon, probably rector of Spaxton, and by William, the rural dean of Ilminster. Richard is in fact the third known deputy archdeacon of Taunton, while two at the same time helped the archdeacon of Wells and one the archdeacon of Bath.

In 1258 Bishop William of Bitton I issued 80 rules for the government of the diocese, from which it is clear that archdeacons and rural deans were both useful and something of a problem. Rural deans were ordered to tell him by the following Easter how many churches they could find that had not been dedicated or about which there was some doubt; they were to take an oath of office to him and not to their archdeacon; and that they and the archdeacons were not to summon people to court without cause and proper inquiry and were not to take money for themselves when parishes were without priests. Yet still in Bishop Droxford's time at the beginning of the fourteenth century rural deans in the Bath area were working for their archdeacon and not their bishop and one, having collected an ancient payment called Peter's Pence on his behalf, was refusing to hand it over.

Bishop Ralph of Shrewsbury, perhaps taking advantage of the chronic absence of archdeacons, agreed with a new archdeacon of Wells in 1338 that he would continue to have the right to hold courts for matters of 'correction' but if the bishop's officer on horseback got to the offender before the archdeacon's officer on foot, then the case would go to the bishop's court. Chaucer was right: 'for er the bisschop caught hem in his hook, they weren in the archedeknes book'. Still, the archdeacon was permitted to deal with all matters of probate provided that the goods of the deceased were entirely within his archdeaconry. Almost certainly by this time rural deans, still chosen annually, no longer acted as collectors for their archdeacon but served as officers of the bishop's courts at Wells, and probably also throughout the diocese. It was a job no-one wanted to do.

The archdeaconry of Glastonbury was different. Here the bishop was kept at arms length thanks to an impudent forgery of the early twelfth century that declared that he should not enter it except by invitation. After much argument he kept the right to hand over spiritual duties in the parishes to new clergy, he alone (or his suffragan) could ordain men from the area and could dedicate new churches. By the 1290s, when those matters were settled, the archdeacon of Glastonbury was carrying out visitations and imposing penances, and his approval was necessary before a candidate for ordination stood before the bishop. The accounts of just one archdeacon, Brother Walter Oscote, have survived for the year 1392-3. His income was quite small: 53s 6d (£2.67p) for visitation fees from the seven churches, 73s 1d (£3.65p) from punishment fines, 66s (£3.30p) from fees for proving wills and 23s (£1.15p) from bequests for making a causeway for which the archdeacon was acting as collector. Among the charges were the expenses of the bishop's officers who seem to have accompanied him on visitation.

Here is a rare glimpse of an archdeacon at work in person, at a time when his colleagues were many miles away from the diocese and their responsibilities. Oscote's successors continued active until the dissolution of Glastonbury in 1539 when their archdeaconry, usually called a jurisdiction, became a deanery within the archdeaconry of Wells. Still, the archdeacons of Wells and Taunton in 1535 took substantial fees from vacant churches, for putting clergy into benefices and for their entertainment allowances at visitations, but only the archdeacon of Wells admitted to fees for proving wills. The archdeacon of Taunton was silent on that matter, perhaps because he had never come to the diocese and the fees went directly to his assistant. That archdeacon was Thomas Cranmer.

The bishop's court, known as his consistory, was much busier. Marriage was seen as integral to settled society and the right to pass possessions from one generation to another was one of the essentials of social stability. The proper payment of money due to the church and its clergy and the sanctity of churches and other things belonging to worship need to be defended. So the bishop's court dealt with such cases. By the end of the Middle Ages the bishop's lawyers held courts every month or so in the cathedral, either in the Lady Chapel by the cloister or when that was being rebuilt in Holy Cross chapel under the north-west tower. By that time a quarter of the cases were to do with marriage, a fifth were for perjury, which included claims for debt interpreted as breach of contract, about a fifth were cases of defamation, though the clerk only once recorded

Ralph of Shrewsbury (bishop 1329-63), bishop during the Black Death. Richard Neale

the actual words by which Robert Vold of North Petherton accused Alice Burode of adultery. And another group of cases involved people not paying money due for all sorts of church charges such as burial fees, tithes and (in the cases of the vicars of Marston Magna, Chilthorne Domer, Doulting and Fivehead) for an increase in stipend in face of inflation.

So the law of the church touched many people. It was designed to encourage the faithful and to correct the defaulter, but its administration was expensive and regular trips to Wells for each case were more than a nuisance. At least the courts dealing with wills were held in many parts of the diocese and were remarkably efficient, protecting the property of the dead from the unwanted attentions of neighbours and quickly handing over administration to executors. There were those, of course, who criticised them as expensive and uncharitable; there were others who found them useful for annoying their neighbours. Almost certainly they saved no souls, though the threat of appearing may well have induced a parishioner to be more faithful and almost certainly produced peaceful solutions in disputes between husband and wife and between parishioners and their priest.

There were other and higher courts to which plaintiffs and defendants at the bishop's courts might appeal - the Court of Arches in London or even to the pope provided, of course, that they had the money or influence to get a hearing. And when the pope was considering all kinds of disputes he recruited bishops, abbots, priors or even archdeacons to make enquiries and come to judgments on his behalf. So, for instance, in 1198 the well-known archdeacon of Bath, Peter of Blois, became involved with the bishop of Rochester and a canon of Wells in a dispute over ownership of several churches in Shropshire and in 1223 Bishop Jocelin and the bishops of Rochester and Salisbury were appointed to settle a quarrel between the bishop of Durham and the monks of his cathedral. More often the problems were more local: in 1345 Bishop Ralph with the bishops of Ely and Durham were ordered to deal with the transfer of a monk to Glastonbury because he had been involved too closely at Eynsham in trouble between two of his brethren who both wanted to be abbot.

In 1398 the prior of Bath was asked to look into the case of two hungry and wandering nuns of Barrow Gurney. His successor in 1442 was asked to intervene between the monks of Hinton and the rector of Norton St Philip who were at odds over finance; whatever agricultural changes had taken place in the meantime, he was to tell both parties that the agreement made in the time of William Marchia was to stand.

The dean of Wells in 1427 found himself the pope's representative in a case that had been heard and decided in the bishop's court. There William Pikwell, rector of Trent (then in the diocese), had been ordered by the judge to do what his predecessors had always done, namely that he should minister to the inhabitants of Over Adber by providing them with a chaplain. The rector clearly

My lord in his castle: Bishop Ralph of Shrewsbury fortified himself and his palace at Wells, possibly before Edward III came to visit in 1331. In the 1340s the buildings included apartments for 'visiting lords' and a prison. Wiltshire and Swindon Record Office 161/142

took no notice of the order and the persistent people of Over Adber took their case to the pope. The pope's instructions to the dean were clear: the rector was to be told to comply, and specifically to find and pay a chaplain to celebrate three times a week and on important festivals in their chapel of St Mary and to provide all sacraments but baptism. How long the chapel, and indeed its people, remained there is not possible to say, but several settlements in neighbouring Mudford seem to have been depopulated not much more than a century later as traditional agricultural practices collapsed. The legal judgments of pope, bishop, dean, or archdeacon could be ignored by personal obstinacy and finally negated by the inexorable march of economic depression.

⌘ ⌘ ⌘

From the very beginning the bishop needed men around him and an income to support his status. Evidently modest at first, there were hints of an adopted grandeur that ill became the pastor but might be expected of the judge. In a real sense the bishop ruled his diocese and was expected to work with its leading landowners as most worked with kings, and land was a necessary demonstration of both social and political position. So gradually estates were acquired and were passed from the bishop to his successor. By 1291 the taxed income of the bishop was nearly £586, modest enough as compared with that of Canterbury, Durham or Winchester (and Glastonbury Abbey) but still enough to attract men already at Salisbury or Exeter, let alone infinitely poorer Welsh bishops. In the mid fifteenth century the bishop's gross income of over £2,000 made Bath and Wells the sixth most valuable see in the country. By 1535 a rather more accurate assessment gave the bishop a net income of just over £1939. What all that meant in reality is revealed in a rare account roll that survives from the time of Ralph of Shrewsbury. Bishop Ralph spent the last few weeks of 1337 and the first of 1338 mostly at his manor houses at Evercreech and Banwell, with trips to the palace at Wells, to Somerton, Cheddar and finally, after a meeting of Parliament in London, to his north Hampshire home at Dogmersfield. Every day he had between 60 and 100 people to feed, and for the few days at Banwell around Old Christmas Day as many as 152. The journey back from London involved 35 riding horses and 18 hackneys carrying luggage; on one night at Dogmersfied 16 gentlemen, 17 officials and 57 servants sat down to dine. The food for the bishop's household was bought locally and included supplies from the bishop's own estates – bacon from Banwell, mutton from Wells, fish from the Axe at Compton Bishop and other goods from Congresbury, Cheddar and Yatton, just a few of his twenty or so manors in Somerset with others in Gloucestershire and Hampshire and a house in London. The names Huish and Kingsbury Episcopi, Bishop's Lydeard and Compton Bishop identify some of them.

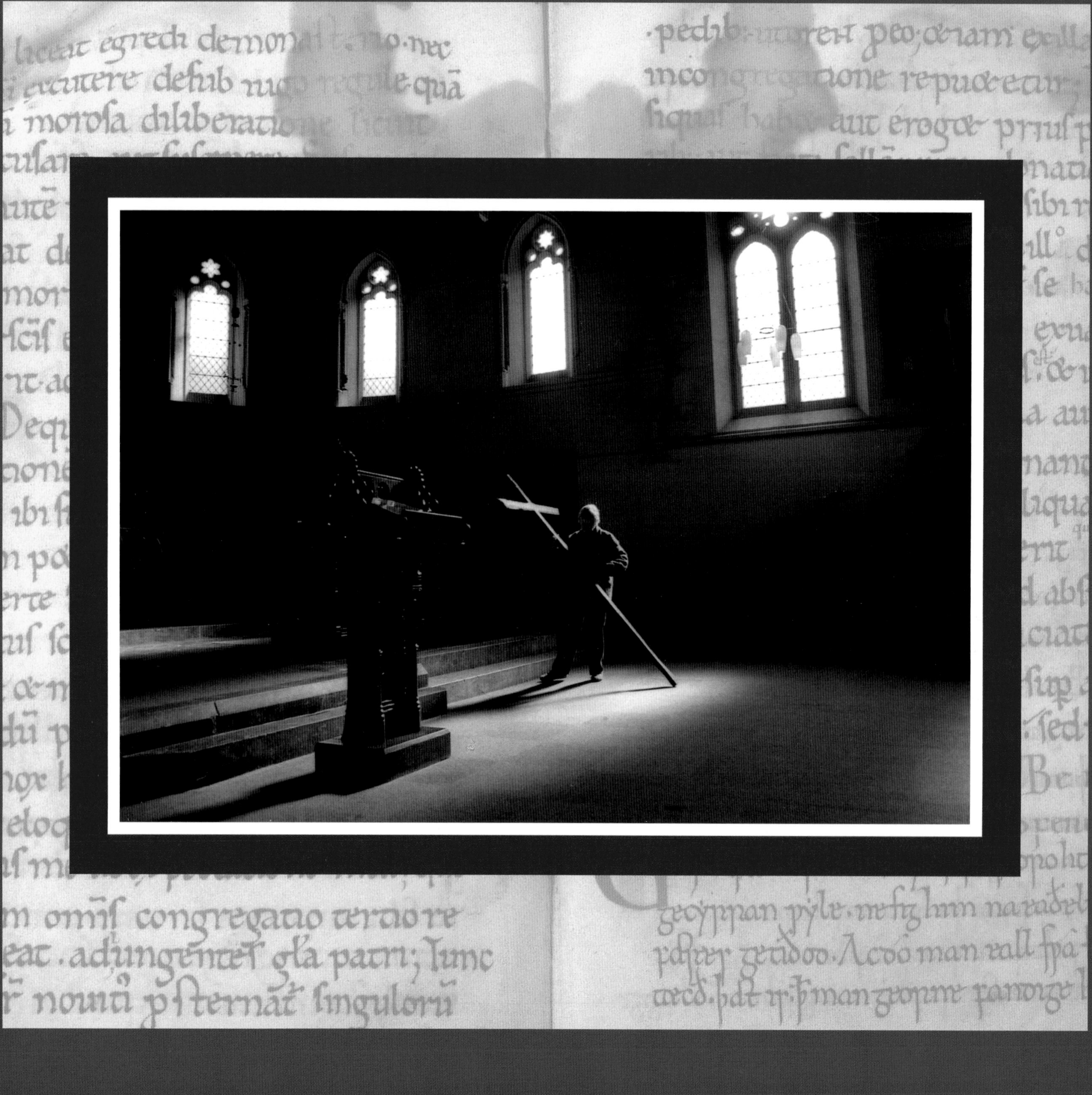

4

From Darkness to Light

Acts 26.18

Into the period of 350 years between the reforms of Pope Innocent III published at the Third Lateran Council in 1215 that Bishop William of Bitton I clearly adopted in his 'Constitutions' and the reforms of Thomas Cranmer, Thomas Cromwell and the Edwardian radicals came the Black Death and the Wycliffite Bible, both with enormous repercussions and both hugely challenging to the church.

THE BLACK DEATH

The single most important event in England in the Middle Ages was announced in the diocese by a circular letter from Bishop Ralph of Shrewsbury to his clergy, sent from his house at Evercreech in mid August 1348. The plague from the East was approaching, he declared, and the clergy were to tell their people - in English so they had no excuse for not understanding - to prepare by confessing their sins, by singing psalms, and by doing works of mercy. When the disease actually arrived in Somerset is not certain, but by the beginning of the second week in November the bishop was safely in his palace at Wiveliscombe and there his registrar recorded the admission of Nicholas Beket as rector of Saltford, replacing one who had evidently died not long before. Several times a week from then until the end of May 1349, and occasionally as many as four times a day, dead rectors and vicars were replaced, in all over 200 or something like a third of the beneficed clergy of the diocese. The rest of the county's population suffered in a similar way and among them were those priests who actually served the parishes and whose lives were at greatest risk as they ministered to the sick and the dying. There is no record of the deaths of such lowly folk.

In the months following that awful visitation the bishop emerged from remote Wiveliscombe and found himself faced with changed and changing communities. There were, inevitably, still parishes and parochial chapels without priests, and neighbouring clergy were brought in, first

Opposite page:
From Darkness to Light.
Phil Day 2004 (© Templar Trust)

47

receiving the bishop's permission to celebrate mass twice on the same day. Michaelchurch was first to admit its plight and the bishop allowed the parish priest of North Newton, or failing him the chaplain at Durston, to celebrate there three times a week. Over the next few months temporary permissions were given for the rector of Barton St David to serve twice a week at West Lydford and then as needed at East Lydford; Dinnington people could have mass on Sundays and feast days said by the rector of Seavington St Michael. Similar arrangements were made for a few months while the rector of Maperton served Blackford, the parish priest of Hemington looked after Writhlington, the vicar of Mudford the chapels of Nether Adber and Hinton. Absence of the rector (in his parish at Prestbury in Gloucestershire) required the chaplain of Leigh on Mendip to celebrate early mass there before high mass at Mells. The arrangement may not have continued when the rector of Mells went off to work for the bishop of Hereford. There is just the suspicion that clergy with influence were taking advantage of the crisis and had actually withdrawn their labour because, as Archbishop Islip put it in a strongly-worded message to the whole province of Canterbury, of 'insatiable greed'.

One or two moves were more radical still. The rector of St Mary Major in Ilchester (the only church in the town now to survive) took over the parish of St Michael le Bowe and also the income of the chantries in his own church (though continuing to say the required masses), and the vicar of Swell was similarly allowed to take over St Katherine's chantry in his church 'long destitute of a priest'. More radical still was the union in 1353 of the parishes of Curry Rivel and Earnshill, the rector of Curry undertaking to find a chaplain to serve Earnshill on Sundays, Wednesdays and Fridays and on the main festivals. Should he be three days late at any service he promised to pay 6s 8d (33p) and costs each time to the cathedral fabric fund and 40d ((16p) to his archdeacon.

A lost village restored: St James, Hambridge, built in 1842 to serve a new community that had grown up at the end of the drive to Earnshill House. Robert Dunning

THE BIBLE IN ENGLISH

As soon as the leading followers of John Wycliffe published their translation of the Bible into English in 1388 people began to study it, as individuals or in groups, and found in it little of the church in which they had been brought up. Lazy and corrupt clergy, forgiveness of sins for cash, a liturgy bordering on the idolatrous and a theology taught by rote and seldom understood was in stark contrast to the simplicity of the church of the apostles and the sure way to salvation preached by Jesus himself. Church authorities were naturally alarmed at such fundamental criticism and the political élite under the Lancastrian kings was with them. An Act of Parliament permitted those who were unwilling to change their radical views to be purged by fire and that same year, 1401, there were rumours of heretical activity in that part of the diocese most difficult to control, namely that part of the city of Bristol outside its walls across the river Avon. And that parish, Bedminster, was an estate attached to Salisbury cathedral and under the immediate control of the holder of that estate, the prebendary of Redcliffe and Bedminster.

Whether such heretical activity was directly associated with people influenced by the English Bible is not known, but for a century and more people from those 'rebel' areas of St Mary Redcliffe, St Thomas and Temple were often in trouble before one bishop or another. When in 1441 Bishop Stafford ordered his archdeacons to search for copies of the Lollard Bible (Lollard from the Dutch word meaning mumblers) he went to the heart of the matter: they contained heresies 'of grave peril to the souls of the simple'. Among those simple, Bishop Stafford and his successors also examined suspects from Frome, Norton St Philip, Beckington, Rode, Holcombe, Leigh on Mendip, Wrington and Taunton (a brewer who actually owned the only book found, but not an heretical one). None ever suffered more than the embarrassment of penitents, for their inquisitors had no wish for blood on their hands and martyrs in their midst.

There were, of course, rogue preachers with fleeting charisma including John Bacon, a chaplain from Stoke Sub Hamdon and more demagogue than heretic. His words had affected ten parishes in the Crewkerne-Ilminster-Langport triangle and so annoyed Bishop Bubwith that he put them all under interdict, thus banning all church activity for a time about 1412. And there was always the possibility that folk religion would prove too attractive. That was Bishop Bekynton's worry in 1464 when the healing properties of a spring at Wembdon suddenly attracted crowds and encouraged offerings to the Virgin and St John the Baptist. The matter was to be investigated with vigour and shut down.

Nevertheless, the confidence of the church had been deeply stirred and Bishop Stafford's teaching programme, however inadequate to many minds a century later, was meant as a wake-up call. For the rest of the century brave individuals emerged from time to time who did not conform in thought or action and the Bible in English was often their inspiration, though nervous authorities were suspicious of any English book as a source of discontent. Religious reformers in the sixteenth century looked back to Wycliffe's Bible as their inspiration, and there was still a persistence of radicalism and, as the mood of the country began to change, an increasing boldness. When a visitation of the diocese was carried out in the king's name in 1537 two men from Temple parish and one from St Mary Redcliffe stood trial: Thomas Mathew of St Mary's 'did take an image and thrust his face in a turd', David Morres of Temple objected to the authority of the King's Visitor, and John Weight, the curate there, concocted his own version of the approved ceremonies in the liturgy. Thomas Amys of Batcombe was thought to hold 'erroneous opinions' but found witnesses to prove the claims false. Far more serious offenders were Thomas Holand of South Cadbury, possessor of a copy of William Tyndale's translation of the New Testament and other suspected heretical books, Thomas Eygges of Buckland Dinham, who read from a copy to his neighbours including a man from Trowbridge, and William Chapman of the same parish who had copies of the Psalter and the Primer in English. The seeds sown by that earlier English Bible were soon to bear much fruit.

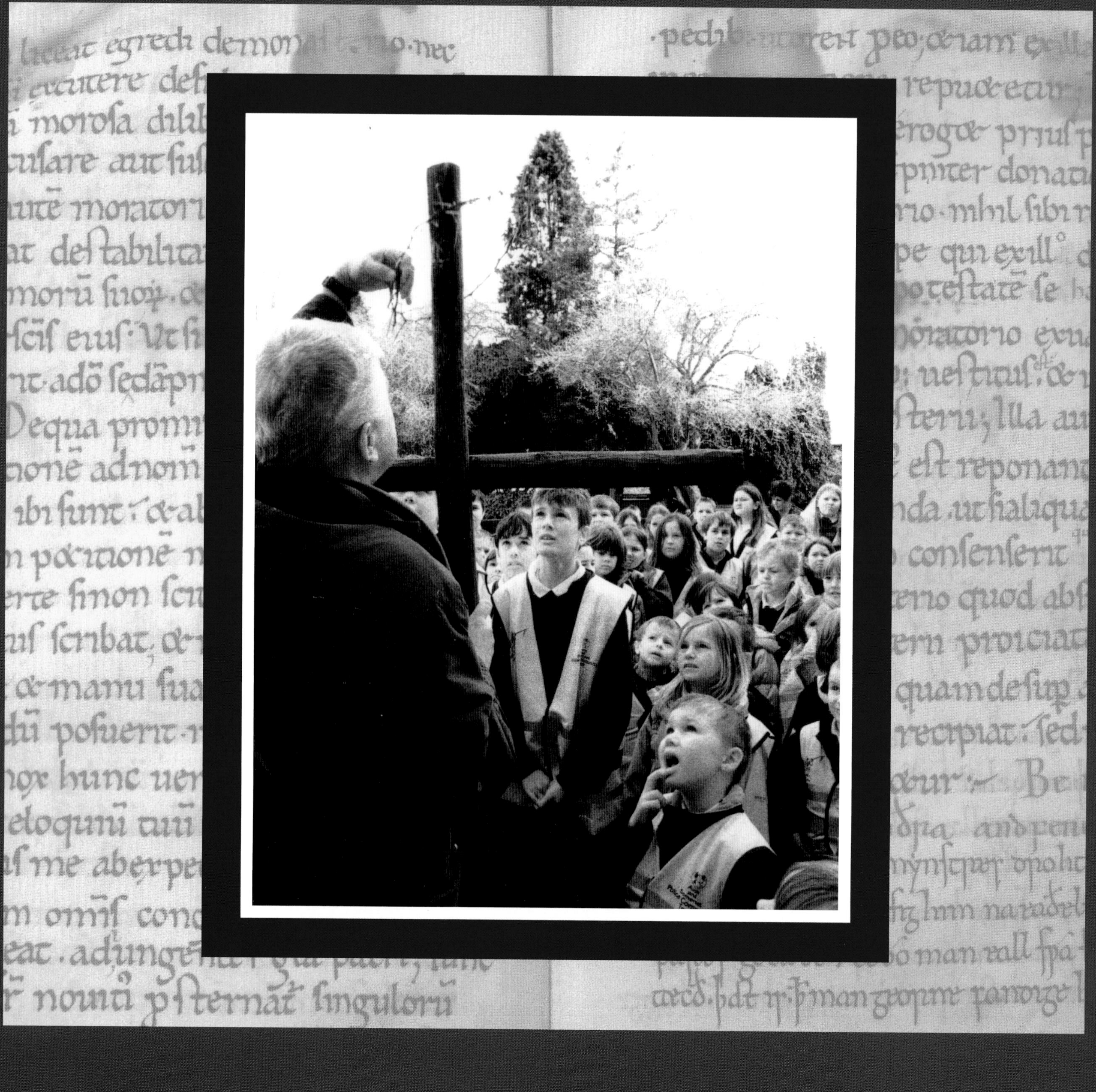

5

Feed My Sheep

John 21. 16,17

Not all the medieval bishops of Bath and Wells were lawyers and civil servants; there were a very few exceptions. Bishop Robert may have been happy to exchange the strict life under the Cluniac Rule at Lewes priory for the more relaxed community at Glastonbury, where Abbot Henry of Blois had called him to bring order and stability, but his creation of the community at Wells showed that he understood how men could work together for a common spiritual purpose. Roger of Salisbury (1243-7), who followed the builder-administrator Jocelin,

Opposite page: Feed my Sheep.
Phil Day 2004 (© Templar Trust)

Tomb of the second William of Bitton (bishop 1267-74).
Michael Blandford (© Dean and Chapter of Wells)

was a theologian and writer who, sadly, had little time to make his mark. William of Bitton I, bishop 1248-64, was something of a reformer although he suffered from the contemporary weakness for appointing members of his large family to positions of authority within the diocese. Pilgrims attracted to the tomb of William of Bitton II, his nephew and bishop 1267-74, in the south choir aisle of the cathedral, found healing, particularly for their toothache, presumably evidence of the bishop's holy and blameless life.

William Marchia, the medieval equivalent of accountant by profession, clearly made an impression of a similar kind at Wells, and over twenty years after his death there was a serious and almost successful attempt to have him

Civil servant and almost-saint: William Marchia (bishop 1293-1302). Michael Blandford (© Dean and Chapter of Wells)

A consecration cross on the south wall of Chedzoy church. Robert Dunning

declared a saint for his unusual humility. To have the tomb of even a modern saint would clearly attract welcome gifts from pilgrims, and the cathedral was in the throes of an expensive building operation, though the cost of the canonisation campaign was found by a tax on all the clergy of the diocese. The death of a sympathetic pope at an inopportune moment ruined the scheme. Ralph of Shrewsbury, who came to Wells as bishop in 1329, was both a church lawyer and a theologian who for a few months around the time of his appointment was also chancellor of Oxford University. His pastoral concerns and spiritual gifts were evident particularly in the way he conducted himself while the Black Death was visited upon his diocese and during its immediate aftermath in 1348-50.

CATHEDRAL AND PARISH CHURCH

Yet whatever their personal attributes and interests, medieval bishops could not avoid the fact that they could not carry out the duties of their office without a care for, and sometimes recourse to, both the law of the church and state and the unanswerable claims of pope and king.

From earliest times to duty of the bishop to set apart a building for the exclusive worship of God had been of the greatest importance, and the builder of the first church at Holcombe in the tenth century had caused the fact to be recorded in stone. Carved consecration crosses on the walls of, for instance, Chedzoy or Moorlinch, permanently record the spot where a bishop had splashed holy water as part of the dedication ceremony. A written record of the ceremony had also to be kept, for the bishop's action had both religious and legal significance. Thus early in 1330 Bishop Ralph of Shrewsbury gave permission for a church to be built in the new village of Shapwick and less than two years later the abbot of Glastonbury, for himself and his successors, promised to indemnify the bishop against any action that might challenge his consecration of the building. In the same rather legalistic fashion 12 parishioners of Henstridge, some six months later, offered themselves as sureties for any actions after the bishop had consecrated their church and four altars inside it. Henstridge church, like Shapwick, was an entirely new building.

Bishop William of Bitton I in the mid thirteenth century had required his rural deans to certify that churches had been consecrated and if there was some doubt they were to report with speed. Clearly, satisfactory answers were not universally received, and fifty years later Bishop Droxford was wrestling with the problem and also with the fact that some clergy were using vessels for the sacraments that had not properly been set aside for their sacred purpose. In a single day some time late in the 1320s Droxford consecrated the churches of East and West Quantoxhead and Kilve, either after rebuilding or simply (and probably more likely) because proof of consecration had not been forthcoming.

Bishop Robert of Lewes in the mid twelfth century had been clear that his newly-reformed college of St Andrew was not to be a place for money changers and salesmen and that those who attended the three traditional fairs were not to bring their business even as far as the porch. Under

Shapwick church, consecrated by Bishop Ralph of Shrewsbury in 1331. Robert Dunning

the reforms of the early thirteenth century the parish churches and their surrounding burial grounds were to be the sacred space of every community, though at Wells but also at, for instance, Axbridge, Bridgwater, Crewkerne and Yeovil, the original market sites were extensions of the churchyard, and the temptation to seek shelter and privacy for business must have been great. Personal distaste for such behaviour or the advent of another general attempt at reform found Bishop Ralph of Shrewsbury ordering the cathedral's dean in 1332 to put an end to trading at fairs both inside the cathedral and in the burial ground

Sacred space thus created could so easily be polluted. In 1311 Bishop Droxford commissioned the bishop of Cork (acting as a suffragan in his absence) to 'reconcile' the parish graveyard at Bruton and both church and graveyard of St Mary Major, Ilchester, both as the result of bloodshed there; and the consequences of pollution were clearly stated after the fracas at St John's, Yeovil. It was, of course, far more than a simple brawl at which someone's nose had been made to bleed. There a crowd armed with bows, arrows, iron bars, stones and anything else they could lay their hands on had confronted Bishop Ralph's servants and in the ensuing fight blood had obviously been spilled. One immediate result was that none could be buried in the churchyard, so for several months corpses had to be taken to either Thorn Coffin or Mudford, a huge and expensive inconvenience.

In his 'Constitutions' issued in 1258 Bishop William of Bitton I provided sensible and probably much-needed rules of behaviour for both clergy and lay people. Unfortunately, church government was nothing if not weighted towards the privileged, and between them pope and king could somehow dispense with almost every means of improvement anyone ever thought of. The bishop had to balance every interest, not least the Common Law of England that regarded the right of a patron to choose a clergyman for his parish as a piece of real property, and such a man once approved by the bishop and put in by an archdeacon was, as a freeholder, very difficult to remove, however unsuitable and unqualified he might be. Perhaps because the bishop's room for manoeuvre had thus become very limited, the 'Constitutions' of Bishop William were not widely known in the diocese. In fact they were re-published in 1343 but there was so much opposition to them from 'some in and of the church of Wells' who thought they would be harmed that in their place Bishop Ralph in 1347 produced some rules of his own. The crisis of the following year probably put paid to much change.

The old vicarage house at Muchelney, in origin a dwelling provided by the monks of Muchelney when the first vicar for the parish was appointed in 1308.
Robert Dunning

RECTORIES AND VICARAGES

By the later twelfth century monasteries, cathedral chapters and other corporate owners of churches had discovered that they could persuade bishops to let them take over (appropriate) the income from those churches, up to that time enjoyed by the rectors they had appointed. Instead of appointing another rector the patrons would receive the income and hire a chaplain to carry out the duties for a minimal sum with no job security. Only a church with a reasonable income, of course, or one still in private ownership, was worth the considerable trouble involved. Bishops, however, usually insisted on a much fairer deal, known as an 'ordination', by which the owner guaranteed a proper income for a vicar, meaning deputy. A vicarage was thus created and among the earliest in the diocese were those of Martock, Old Cleeve, Somerton and North Petherton, involving respectively Otterton priory, Cleeve abbey, Muchelney abbey and Buckland priory.

The pace of change quickened by the later thirteenth century so that by 1291 there were at least 45 vicarages in the diocese compared with 240 rectories. More were to follow, seven in Bishop Droxford's time between 1308 and 1327. A few were created in the fifteenth century and one of the last, Crewkerne, not until 1547. By that time the remaining rectories were usually very poor and hardly worth dividing; many were worth less than vicarages. Some sort of order had thus at last been achieved, and when in some parishes economic circumstances changed, the ordination of a vicarage could be altered. That was done, for instance, at Winsford in 1453 because the vicar found he had not enough land on which to keep the animals that came to him in payment of tithes. In the following year it was agreed at Stockland Bristol that the arable lands of the parish had been converted to grass and the value of the vicar's grain tithe was drastically reduced. At Evercreech the same seems to have been the case, sheep grazing there taking over from arable and causing the depopulation of the hamlets of Chesterblade, Southwood and Bagborough.

RECTORS, VICARS AND PARISH PRIESTS

About one quarter of Bishop William's 'Constitutions' referred to the lifestyles of clergy. Priests were not, for instance, to keep concubines, not to drink in taverns or at parties, not to become involved with secular business, not to go hunting or fishing, not to fine people after hearing their confessions. They were to wear sober clothes and behave properly, and archdeacons were to enquire how many were not very literate.

When Richard of Woodbury was appointed vicar of Brompton Regis in 1315 he was specifically examined in 'literature', that is his ability to read. William of Brumpton, appointed rector of Walton in Gordano in 1321, was found to be both young and 'ignorant' and there were very many like him in the first half of the fourteenth century. William was ordered to study and to nominate a chaplain to serve the parish, for he would not only be absent for a year at least but he was not even an acolyte, the lowest of the major holy orders and thus quite unable to celebrate mass. As part of the whole arrangement William also had to provide money to help needy scholars.

The general standard of education of clergy had improved by the next century, and a man with ability and a patron could get a university degree. An outstanding example was Bishop Thomas Bekynton himself. The clever son of a Beckington weaver, he was somehow found a place at Winchester college and went on to New college, Oxford, eventually becoming one of the pioneering humanist scholars of the time. His active support of both the song school and the grammar school at Wells and the circle of scholars he gathered around him, both as cathedral canons and parish priests, was a measure of his concern for the still unsatisfactory level of education of many clergy. Yet so keen were men to take holy orders that a few suffered the embarrassment of failing examination. Ordaining bishops were amazingly kind to a few who revealed deplorable shortcomings. William Northron, a vicar choral, would have lost his job had he not been made subdeacon on 24 March 1459, and it was only by 'special grace' of the bishop that he was accepted and promised the bishop's chancellor, on oath, 'that he would diligently study to learn grammar and acquire an understanding of the scripture, especially at such times as he could be absent from the cathedral choir'. There was no such comment when he was made deacon just under a year later, but six months after that, when he presented himself to be priested, he was examined again by the

Bishop Bekynton usually used a 'rebus' instead of a coat of arms displayed in the Penniless Porch at Wells. It shows a tun (barrel) fixed on top of a pole to create a beacon. Jerry Sampson

same chancellor and a theologian. There is more than a suspicion that Northron either had not applied himself or had failed to get study leave from the choir, for against his name in the bishop's register of ordinations are the words *ex gracia*. Perhaps a lesson had been learnt by the authorities: on that same occasion Thomas Popham of Stogumber, also priested, 'swore on the Gospels to do his utmost to attain a better knowledge and understanding of grammar' and agreed to present himself on a given day at the bishop's court each year 'until he be capable'. One or two other ordination candidates around the same time made similar promises.

An adequate income was important for every parish priest, but from the point of view of parishioners there were more pressing issues. Bishop William had ordered that within a month or two of the publication of his 'Constitutions' vicars should actually live on their parishes or lose their posts unless they had 'good and honest cause' to be absent. Rectors, on the other hand, were simply 'urged' to reside and to think of their parishioners. The difference was simply that the bishop imagined he had more power over the one than the other, but in effect Bishop William and his successors were hard put to it to raise standards, for popes and kings were for ever intervening on behalf of clergy they wanted to reward or employ, removing them from the parishes they were appointed to serve by offering them more attractive employment elsewhere. The bishop might take great care when accepting a man for a post, first, that it was legally vacant, and second that the patron, the one nominating the candidate, was the true and lawful one. Those phrases are still found in the services of institution and induction today. The bishop's registrar then recorded each appointment with great care, and often enough in the fourteenth century he noted in cases of some doubt that the bishop had insisted on insurance to protect himself from possible legal action.

Absence to serve the king or someone else of importance was considered entirely legitimate, so there was no problem for the bishop when Robert de Sarr, rector of Bratton St Maur, sought leave to serve the bishop of Exeter and when the rector of Bleadon went off for a year to wind up the estate of the late bishop of Winchester, both in 1311, or when in 1312 the rector of Marksbury was allowed to go for a year in the king's service, in 1317 when the rector of Charlcombe went to work for Sir Roger de Felton or in 1319 when the rector of Chedzoy went to serve the patron, Sir William de Montacute, far away in Gascony where he was the king's seneschal. In the event Sir William died at Bordeaux a few months later, so presumably the rector returned to his parish.

Study leave was another entirely legitimate reason for the absence of rectors and vicars, one or two of whom, like the three Pykeslegh brothers, rectors respectively of Hutton, Weston super Mare and Backwell, amassed between them at least 20 years legal absence. Many young newly-appointed men went off to university almost as a matter of course, the parish income in effect forming their university grant. The only control Bishop Droxford was able to exercise was to order his staff to check all absentees, for he had heard that some young men had left their studies and gone to London where they behaved disgracefully 'to the decay of hospitality and almsgiving in their parishes', a phrase that summed up well what was actually expected of a rector or vicar at the time - to be sociable to their equals and generous to the rest.

There were other legitimate reasons for being away. The vicar of Bridgwater in 1318 and the rector of Bleadon in 1319 went on pilgrimage to Canterbury, the rector of Mells and Bagborough together ventured to Compostella, the rector of Oare was given the period from August to Christmas to go to Avignon and back, and Simon de Lym, vicar of St Mary's, Taunton, had made a vow to go to unnamed foreign shrines as well as having business at the papal court. And absence, as Bishop Droxford figured several times, might make the heart grow fonder. William of Bath, rector of Swainswick, left his parish for two years from 1318 'because of the ill-will of his flock', and Robert of Upton left Shepton Beauchamp for a while 'on account of parochial strife', though apparently not of his making.

How, therefore, in face of such frequent and extended absences, did the work of the church survive for much of the Middle Ages? It was thanks to an underclass of priests without the advantages of birth and influence, who led worship, taught the faith and took pastoral care in parish after parish. When the first vicar of Burnham was appointed in 1336 it was agreed as a matter of course that he would appoint and pay a chaplain to serve in the church. A rare testimonial written by Bishop Ralph in 1333 paid tribute to Richard David who had served as parish priest at Wellington for 24 years without a break. Where he and his like came from is not often recorded, but both Bishop Droxford and Bishop Ralph freed serfs born on their estates so that they might become priests to serve in the diocese. William and Agnes Batyn of Bathampton were no doubt delighted and proud that Bishop Droxford not only freed Adam, one of their five sons, and in 1311 personally conferred on him the first tonsure, the first step in a clerical career, and promised him future promotion should he prove suitable. Adam Roules of Wick St Lawrence, another of the bishop's serfs but described as a poor scholar who had somehow managed to get an education, was similarly freed and tonsured in 1325, but there were strings attached. Should he become a priest he would have to be one of those anonymous men who served in a Somerset parish while his rector or vicar enjoyed their official status and left him to it.

Such a system still continued for at least a century. When all clergy, of whatever status, were taxed in 1450 their names appear in Bishop Bekynton's register. In the list from Dunster deanery are parish chaplains from Porlock, Wootton Courtney, Winsford, Luxborough, Carhampton, Williton, Tolland and Fitzhead, a chantry priest at Dunster and a chaplain celebrating anniversary masses at Watchet. With the exception of Richard God at Porlock, who doubled up as rector of Oare, none appears in the official lists of men ordained by the bishop or his predecessors. Those were second-class mass priests able to perform all the services the church required, but men of little or no social status. These were the priests, often referred to by people making their last wills as 'my curate', who knew their people as pastor and friend as no absentee rector or vicar could possibly have done. These were the priests who kept the faith alive in the parishes.

TEACHING AND LEARNING

The Fourth Lateran Council in 1215 reminded bishops that they had a crucial teaching role; the seats they each occupied in their cathedrals were by origin the stools of a teacher rather than the thrones of a ruler, but priorities and attitudes of bishops had evidently changed. By the 1140s there were two schools at Wells that Bishop Robert of Lewes wanted to protect and strengthen, one under the precentor and the succentor limited to choristers, the other a grammar school, the responsibility of the *archischola* or chancellor and by about 1200 run by a schoolmaster. The grammar school, which from the beginning taught some of the youths closely associated with the liturgy as the beginning of a clerical career, clearly thrived and by the end of the fourteenth century perhaps had up to 70 pupils. The chancellor, relieved of his duties to the young, probably turned, as in Exeter and Salisbury, to higher study for local clergy unable to go to university. Bishop Ralph discovered about 1335 that the then chancellor had for years neglected to give the traditional lectures on church law or theology, nor had he found someone else to give them. Typically, the bishop-theologian recently down from Oxford insisted that the lectures be reinstated between mid October and early July each year, a period that sounds very much like an academic year. Unfortunately, chancellors came and went at the time with some frequency and teaching probably suffered. A century later the theologian John Orum lectured at Wells on the Apocalypse, perhaps deputizing for the then chancellor.

The Council of Lambeth of 1281 had laid down the view that the duty of the laity was to have some knowledge of the Ten Commandments, the Seven Works of Mercy, the Seven Virtues, the Seven Deadly Sins and the Seven Sacraments. Such knowledge, acquired by as much teaching as the parish priest could manage, was reinforced by the powerful imagery on view in most churches and was a sure pathway to heaven. In 1435 Bishop Stafford spelled out that national curriculum at great length for his clergy, probably conscious of the pressure created by those, notably in Bristol's suburbs, who through reading the Bible had come to a radically different view. So he ordered his clergy to rehearse the teaching programme four times a year 'openly in English ... without curious subtlety'. Acceptance by the people would, with God's help and the bishop's earnest encouragement, bring salvation.

The pulpit at Long Sutton, dating from the late 1450s and bearing the initials of both rector (the abbot of Athelney) and vicar.
Robert Dunning

Scene from the life of the Virgin: the Dormition (sleep) at Sutton Bingham. Hugh and Bridget Playfair

There was at least one other way to teach the faith. In her will dated 24 January 1503 Agnes Burton or Bascombe gave generously to St Mary's, Taunton, and among her bequests was a silk-lined cloak, a white shift and a silver-gilt box 'to thentent of Mary Magdaleyn play'. That play, according to an expert on the history of drama, was 'a semi-liturgical play' about the Resurrection involving Christ the gardener and the patron saint of the church. Religious drama was an important feature in the life of many churches, and at least from the 1320s until 1538 the cathedral marked the feast of the Holy Innocents by creating a liturgy around a boy bishop and some accompanying 'canons', the whole affair ending with a celebration that cost 2s 9d (14p). There was, of course, a fine line between religious drama and pure entertainment, and the cathedral's junior clergy who marked the previous week around Christmas Day with 'plays contrary to the decency of the church ... bringing in the likeness of ghosts ... [and] presume to use the mockeries of their madness' were roundly admonished. Towards the end of the fourteenth century the commemoration of a former canon on the feast of the Conception of the Virgin was accompanied by a procession including the boy bishop and by the early fifteenth century a play was performed in Easter week involving the Holy Saviour and pilgrims, and another on Easter Eve with the three Marys.

Plays were performed probably in many parish churches to bring the faith alive. At Bridgwater, Glastonbury and Yeovil performances were staged at Corpus Christi and at Christmas at Glastonbury and Tintinhull according to the few surviving churchwardens' accounts. Bridgwater also had a shepherd's pageant, Yatton welcomed minstrels at Whitsun, and St Michael's, Bath, in 1482 hosted players 'on divers occasions', providing them with food, drink and materials for props, and on several occasions rented out a crown, once each for the use of the parishes of Saltford and

Right: *The brass lectern in St John's, Yeovil, dating from about 1450 and perhaps given by or in memory of Brother Martin Forester. At the time of its making it would have been used by the priest conducting services, not for holding a bible.* Hugh and Bridget Playfair

Far right: *St Christopher in Ditcheat church.* Hugh and Bridget Playfair

Swainswick perhaps for some religious purpose, and regularly for the city's secular celebration of the summer king at Whitsun. Thus feasts of the church were brought to the notice of young and old, and like the regular round of services within the church building where action, colour, light and music together could play on the imagination of the uneducated and the illiterate.

THE FAITH OF THE FLOCK

However acquired, and whether more of the heart than the head, the faith of the flock was real and active. It was expressed in many ways, but how is personal piety to be found? The popularity of pilgrimage, already noted among the clergy in the early fourteenth century, clearly continued in the 15th and there were evidently regular sailings from Bristol and Southampton for travel to the shrine of St James at Compostella both direct to Spain or via Talmont near Bordeaux. A busy merchant like Gilbert Russell of Bridgwater somehow never found the time to travel in person but in his will of 1317 left 40s (£2) for someone to go to Compostella and Rocamadour and 10s (50p) to another to visit the holy rood at Bromholm priory, the holy house at Walsingham and the shrine of St Thomas at Canterbury. Three much less prominent folk went in person from Minehead to Canterbury in 1378 and over twenty years later remembered that a local landowner's son was baptised just before they left.

People were often attracted to the unusual and it was often as well to test its worth. The value of the water by the Lady Chapel at Glastonbury abbey was so obvious that Abbot Bere constructed a chapel beneath it and positively welcomed visitors. The statue of the Virgin in the chapel beneath the cliff near what is now Blue Anchor was long a place of pilgrimage and its safety when the chapel was destroyed in 1452 only served to prove its sanctity. Its popularity caused the abbot of Cleeve to build a hostel for pilgrims, and parts of it still survive though both statue and chapel had gone by the 1540s. Other holy objects in the diocese in the years before the Reformation included a painted or carved image of the Trinity at Bath and the images of or chapels dedicated to the Saviour at Porlock, Taunton, Bradford and Bridgwater.

CHANGING COMMUNITIES

Christmas, Easter, Pentecost, Corpus Christi were the best known among the fifty or so holy days of the liturgical year when the parish community could come together in their sacred space or move together in procession in theatrical expression of their faith. None locally was so important as their dedication festival, not the day of their patron saint but the day when, however many years ago it may have been, the bishop came to set their church apart. The reformers had insisted that such ceremony took place and gradually altars and sacred vessels were also blessed, fonts were covered and locked, and oil and chrism kept safely. Secular activities such as markets were also excluded. Bishop Droxford made sure that the people of Burnham were in no doubt of the significance of the event when in 1315 he went to Burnham church, then rebuilt from its foundations. He ordered them to keep the festival each year and offered right-thinking visitors indulgences of 40 days in response for their offerings.

So each dedication festival became a significant part of the parish calendar, the main occasion apart from Christmas and Easter for the collection of offerings. It was the day (the feast of the 11000 virgins) when the churchwardens of St Michael's in Bath opened their accounts each year. In the course of time, however, some parishes found that better results might be had if the day were changed. The people of Shapwick struggled for success because their festival (St Edith 16 Sept.) usually fell on a working day in the middle of harvest or winter ploughing and in 1464 requested it be moved just a few days to the Sunday after the feast of the Exaltation of the Holy Cross. A few years earlier, in 1439, the people of St Matthew's, Wookey, were allowed to changed their dedication feast from the octave of the Nativity of the Virgin (8 September) to the Sunday after St Jerome (30 September) for exactly the same reasons. Similar changes were made at Croscombe, West Monkton, Kingstone, Kingsdon, Weston (which?), Kewstoke, Norton sub Hamdon and West Cranmore, nearly always in favour of a Sunday.

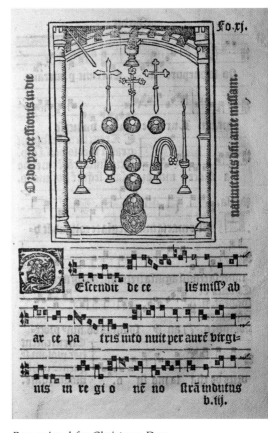

Processional for Christmas Day before mass. Michael Blandford (© Dean and Chapter of Wells)

Changes of dedication feasts demonstrate the pressure on agriculture that was a feature of the later Middle Ages. Another, and more radical change, was to bring poor parishes together to provide an adequate income for the priest. Woodwick was united with Freshford in 1448 and Fairoak with Berkley in 1460 and the united parishes of St Mary Minor and St John, Ilchester, with the parish of St Mary Major there in 1502. A plan to join Hardington with Laverton was not carried out.

Yet not all was contraction in changing communities. The village of Coleford, at the southern edge of Kilmersdon parish, was clearly growing, perhaps as a result of increasing coal mining. In 1476 the bishop recognised the growth and gave permission for services to be held there, a mission church in a busy parish. Another unusual arrangement was made in the heart of the Levels in 1515. There the busy and populous parish was divided into three parts at the initiative of the vicar of what was up to then called Sowy or Weston in Sowyland and with the support of four men each from Weston, Middlezoy and Othery. The vicar declared formally that the two chapels were well supported and there would be quite enough money and land to support two new vicarages. The new vicars, typical of the time, were graduates and priests; curious was the new appointment to Weston, who was only a deacon and thus would have to employ a priest-chaplain.

A page from a late-thirteenth-century breviary from a parish church for the feast of St Sebastian. Preserved because used as cover for an account book of the Bridgwater water bailiff. Blake Museum, Bridgwater. (Somerset Record Office DD/BLM 10/3)

St Mary's, Taunton, was almost too busy. Probably in the 1420s a set of rules had been drawn up by the then archbishop of Canterbury, but Bishop Bekynton in his first visitation found that a certain laxity had set in, for chaplains had been wandering around the nave, 'paying attention' to the walls and windows, or simply absenting themselves in the churchyard or their own lodgings when their own duties were complete, rather than attending to the continuing services. The problem was that three chantry chaplains and five others had somehow to be allowed to say or sing their masses while the main daily services in the choir 'beginning at the fifth or sixth hour in the dawn' and proceeding much as in the cathedral or monastic churches with lauds, matins, sometimes prime, and high mass. A mass was sung every day in the Lady chapel and the bishop decreed that the other masses should be fitted in with proper dignity at specified times, the first at the beginning of lauds, the second immediately after matins and so on to produce 'successive' masses. On Sundays and feast days worship was to be concentrated in the choir where the beginning of the Lady mass would be signalled up to a quarter of a mile away by a bell. There the vicar 'if his cure permits' and the other priests 'in the absence of any lawful and urgent excuse' were to worship together vested only in surplice and cap unless ill health or extreme cold demanded hoods.

That little religious community continued, hopefully along the improved lines required. By

1548 the number of chantries had grown to six and two fraternities had been established providing continuing prayers for their members. It was among the busiest parish churches of the diocese alongside St John's, Frome, St Mary's, Bridgwater, and St Cuthbert's, Wells (where there had been the vicar and 13 chaplains and clerks in 1377 but only the vicar, a chantry chaplain and two other chaplains in 1548). St Mary Redcliffe, remarkably not a parish church, was probably busier still, but it left the diocese for Gloucester in 1541.

The wills of the people of St Mary's, Taunton, from the 1480s onwards reveal an anxiety to do the right thing by their parish church both as a sacred space where in life their faith might be demonstrated and in death their memory might be recorded. Thanks to such generosity a fine south aisle and other space were created for processions, an impressive porch marked the entry into a glimpse of heaven and a tower built to stand as a symbol of their aspirations and a demonstration of their prosperity. Church building across the diocese from the fourteenth century onwards was at the heart of the activity of nearly every parish and the money to pay for it, a clear reflection of both economic prosperity and religious commitment, involved every section of parish society. The key fundraiser was the production of ale, called simply a brewing at Tintinhull,

Figures on the three faces of the south porch at Curry Rivel, perhaps all three replacements, but strongly suggesting that its upper room might have served as a musicians' gallery. Jerry Sampson

Three church houses.
Above: *Chew Magna.*
Top right: *Crowcombe.*
Right: *Croscombe.*
Robert Dunning

Goathurst and St Michael's, Bath, church ale in most places. It was sometimes linked with bread as at Nettlecombe where it was called hoggling bread (for labourers); it was tavern ale at Yatton, Roodmasse ale at Halse and Trull, All Saints ale, also at Trull, brewing at Petertide at North Curry and Pentecost ale at Stogursey and Williton. For fund-raising in the later Middle Ages was all about celebration and mild rivalry. At Glastonbury in 1500 the wives and young women seem to have taken on the task of gilding the statue of St George, leaving men to organise the much larger one of funding the new seats ordered from a Bristol carver. Their method was to divide the parish into districts and have a collector for each armed with a 'croke' to accept gifts in cash or kind. At Croscombe in the 1470s and 1480s the weavers, the tuckers, the hogglers (farm labourers), the young men, the maidens and the dancing wives, with the useful support of Robin Hood all did their share. The ubiquitous Robin Hood with dancing girls and church ale was active at St Cuthbert's, Wells, and 'by his good persuasion and diligent labours' and the 'good devotion of the town and country' at Yeovil raised over £6 in 1519.

The treasury and vestry at Croscombe, built between 1496 and 1513 and the meeting place of the parish guilds. Robert Dunning

The purpose of all this activity was essentially practical: the maintenance and improvement of the parish church and what went on inside it, all for the glory of God and not a little local satisfaction. And since bishops had from the fourteenth century discouraged the use of the church building for secular purposes, some other venue had to be found. The answer in much of South-West England was the church house, a building where bread might be baked, ale brewed and parties enjoyed, all for the benefit of the parish church, financial and social. The church houses at Chew Magna, Croscombe and Crowcombe are obvious survivors of hundreds across the diocese, most on manorial land on the edge of churchyards, but others some distance away, like the one on Abdick Green in Ilton parish. The church house provided space to have the inevitable and probably welcome parish party to which neighbouring parishes were invited: the Goathurst wardens went to Broomfield, Durleigh and Wembdon, the Tintinhull folk to Chilthorne Domer, Montacute and Stoke Sub Hamdon. Had there been such a place in Wembdon in 1325 when the rebuilding of the church had become essential, there would have been no need for the imposition of a rate throughout the parish and therefore no need for Bishop Droxford to send the rural dean of Bridgwater to threaten non-payers with dire recriminations. Amazingly, such attitudes were rare. Parishioners like those of Doulting in 1332 might refuse to pay tithes, a common enough complaint until tithes were abolished; but such refusal was as much to do with personal objections to the clergy or economic problems. A parish party was no imposition.

6

Your Word is a Lamp

Psalm 119. 105

Olive, crown and mitre: Bishop Oliver King's rebus on the west front of Bath Abbey. Robert Dunning

The bishops who ruled the diocese between 1466 and 1494, Robert Stillington and Richard Fox, were both politicians and civil servants intimately connected with royal service. Oliver King, who came to the diocese in 1496, was in the same mould, royal secretary and something of a vicar of Bray, for he served Lancastrian, Yorkist and Tudor kings and princes. But in his short stay (he died in 1503) he made one particular mark: the west front of Bath Abbey portrays ladders with angels climbing up and down, and on each ornate buttress an olive tree with a crown around its trunk surmounted by a bishop's mitre. Here is the visual reminder of the local legend that Bishop King had a dream while staying in the city when a voice declared 'let an olive establish the crown, let a king restore the church'. The new church was planned as part of a complete rebuilding and reformation of the whole abbey.

King was followed as bishop by Hadrian de Castello, a native of Corneto in Italy but a naturalised Englishman. He had worked in this country since 1489 as collector of papal taxes but from 1500 he was living in Rome where he represented Henry VII at the papal court. He was made bishop of Hereford in 1502, a cardinal in 1503, and bishop of Bath and Wells in 1504. He is known to have been in London in 1507 and 1508 and in Wells in 1510 and 1513, but the diocese was regarded by him as simply a source of income; its administration he was happy to leave to others. His own career outside England was a roller-coaster, at one time spoken of as the next pope, in 1518 deprived both of his bishopric and his office as cardinal. His successor was Thomas Wolsey, already archbishop of York and a rather busy man.

Opposite page: *Your Word is a Lamp.* Phil Day 2004 (© Templar Trust)

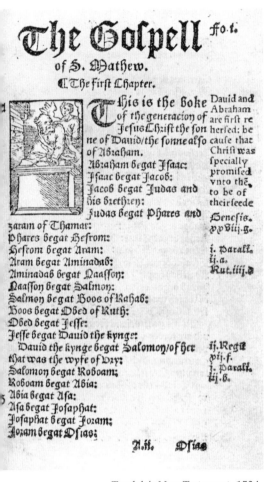

Tyndale's New Testament, 1534.

William Tyndale, born in Gloucestershire in the 1490s and returning there in the 1520s, complained that most of the clergymen he knew understood 'no more what the Old or New Testament meant than do the Turks; neither know they any more than they read at mass, matins and evensong, which they understand not'. John Hooper, once a monk at Cleeve abbey, was amazed when he was appointed bishop of Gloucester in 1550 to find that over half his clergy could not repeat the Ten Commandments and some were unable to recite the lord's prayer or tell who its author was. Gloucestershire and Somerset were neighbours and there is little reason to suppose that its clergy were much different. Yet Tyndale and Hooper were two among hundreds of thousands who were profoundly affected by the religious movements, beginning on the continent, which together inspired what is generally called the Reformation.

Criticism of the clergy and their standards of learning and behaviour was not new: the laws of the Anglo-Saxon kings so many years before had assumed that perfection was seldom achieved without pressure and encouragement, and the writings of contemporary church leaders like Aelfric had implied the same. Many medieval bishops had taken improving measures, evidently with limited success, but the popularity of the Lollard Bible had shown the vital importance of the scriptures available in a native language. And that was precisely Martin Luther's purpose in trans-lating the Bible into his own native tongue and Tyndale in his. Luther wanted 'to make Moses so German that no-one would suspect he was a Jew'; Tyndale hoped 'to cause a boy that driveth the plough' to know more of the scriptures than the bishop of London. Luther's translation, like the famous statement he nailed to the church door in Wittenberg, as intended to reform the church he loved; instead they began a revolution. Tyndale's unfinished translation inspired a complete and officially sanctioned version by Miles Coverdale in 1535 and inspired 'a veritable era of bible-making'; culminating in the Authorized Version or King James Bible in 1611. By that time both bishops of London and ploughboys knew a great deal about the Word of God, but the revolution which had been brought about in its understanding was to have far-reaching consequences. The right if not the duty of individuals to interpret the Bible for themselves allowed them also the right to reject the interpretations of others. The century-and-a-half after Luther's defiant action was to see the church in England seriously at odds with itself.

THE ENGLISH CHURCH IS BORN

The gradual revelation of the Word of God came to a kingdom ruled by a prince whose education had inclined him to be theologically conservative but whose opinion might change according to political pressure. Henry VIII's desperate need for a male heir, and hence an annulment or divorce, brought in question the power of the pope (not a new idea, for kings of England had often clashed with popes, especially about the choice of bishops) and the attractive prospect of bishops and clergy entirely under the king's control.

Henry VIII's chief minister for more than ten years until his death in 1529 was Thomas Wolsey, a man of great ability whose career was an extreme example of the corruption of senior clergy. Between 1518 and 1523 he somehow managed to be both archbishop of York and bishop of Bath and Wells and also Lord Chancellor, head of the king's government. He never, of course, returned to Somerset as bishop where long ago in his youth he had been resident rector of Limington and is said to have been put in the stocks after being found drunk and disorderly.

The failure of Wolsey to find a solution to the king's marital problems was followed by an attack on the church of which as papal legate he had been leader. A series of measures supported by a sympathetic parliament over the next fifteen years radically changed the position of both that church and its clergy. At the head of the reformers in this period of 'tempestuous uncertainties' was Thomas Cranmer, whose work over the king's problem had also proved unsuccessful but whose reward was to be appointed archbishop of Canterbury in 1532. He was essentially an academic by training, had been a parish priest in only one place but nominally archdeacon of Taunton. He, too, almost certainly never came to Somerset; he was far too busy meeting German reformers on the king's business. While abroad he also met a lady whom he married and kept very quiet about for several years. Supporting Cranmer during that time were new reformist bishops including Hugh Latimer of Worcester and Nicholas Ridley, then of Rochester and later of London. Opposed to them still were men of the old school, the most senior Richard Nix, bishop of Norwich, a Somerset man who had been for a time rector of High Ham, and Stephen Gardiner, bishop of Winchester. And there were, of course, Somerset clergy who thought the same, perhaps none so outspoken as John Divale, curate of Wincanton, who called all who read the English scriptures 'heretics and knaves and Pharisees, and likened them to a dog that gnaweth on a mary [marrow] bone' and said he hoped 'to see the bishop of Worcester burned, with all the new books in England about him'.

Those fifteen years, and particularly the first five, were revolutionary, for they saw the church brought entirely under the control of the state, with the king at its head. Acts of Parliament and Royal Injunctions came so thick and fast they must have been hugely disturbing and confusing, particularly to hard-pressed churchwardens in every parish who had to find money to pay for the changes demanded. At the same time each bishop had to maintain his staff and courts, for he was still the pastor of his flock and the judge of their iniquities.

⊞ ⊞ ⊞

The conquest of the church began in December 1530 when the clergy, who had accepted Wolsey as the pope's representative in England, were accused of treason for doing so and found themselves in their own assembly (Convocation) offering the king a large sum of money to overlook the

VI. COVERDALE BIBLE, 1535.

Above: *Coverdale Bible, 1535.*

Above right: *Lectern, Monksilver, quite old enough to have held a Coverdale Bible.* Robert Dunning

matter. In addressing him as 'protector and only supreme Head of the English Church ... as far as the law of Christ allows' they replaced the pope with the king, and by a series of almost bewildering measures Henry VIII made himself not just titular but actual head of the Church of England, removing all traces of papal authority and transferring to his own pocket the large sums of money bishops used to send to Rome on appointment. Henceforth clergy were obliged (as they still are) to take an oath of loyalty to the sovereign, and in a series of enquiries the finances of each clergyman and every monastery were recorded and the activities of each monastery were investigated.

Such a programme of legislation was as much nationalistic as reformist and was approved of by traditionalists and reformers alike, but the Statute of the Six Articles published in 1539 showed how little headway Cranmer and his fellow radicals had made. Its purpose was to abolish 'diversity in opinion' by declaring that, whatever arguments to the contrary, the bread and wine at consecration was the substance of Christ, that communion in both kinds was not necessary, that priests were not to marry, that vows of chastity were to be accepted, that private masses were allowed and confession to a priest was 'expedient'. A conservative king was unwilling to go further and his ministers and bishops were not allowed to overtake him. Yet by that time the monasteries had disappeared without much opposition - though three of the martyrs were Glastonbury monks - and the Bible in English, Coverdale's completion of the work of Tyndale, was published with the king's licence in 1537. Its revision, known as the Great Bible, was ordered to be set up in churches for free and public reading in 1539. That important change cost the churchwardens of Yatton the large sum of 9s 6d (48p) 'for a bybyll'; Trull parish bought the large version for 18s 4d (92p) with another 4d for a chain and cover, but had to borrow half the sum. Someone was making money; a Royal Injunction in 1541 reduced the cost to 10s (50p) unbound.

There is not much indication in the official records of John Clerke and William Knight, bishops between 1523 and 1547, that the diocese was anything but traditional in outlook and practice. Both bishops, after all, were typical of their time, both lawyers by training and diplomats by employment. Clerke had been closely associated with Wolsey's schemes in Rome, Knight in his early career with missions to Spain, Italy and the Low Countries. Clerke only came to Somerset occasionally, drew up his will when taken ill at Dunkirk while on a mission to Cleves, but died in London and was buried there, leaving money for prayers for his souls at Wells, Banwell and Chew. Knight wished to be buried in his cathedral and left money for the poor on all his estates, though Wiveliscombe was evidently his favourite and he left the tapestries in his great dining room there to a friend. The cathedral's Renaissance-style pulpit, certainly not built from any bequest by him, would seem to be an odd memorial to such a traditionalist.

The bishop might be absent, but the work of the diocese went on. The administrative work of holding the courts, administering wills and putting clergy into parishes was carried out by his legal staff. Suffragan or visiting bishops ordained clergy and consecrated churches, churchyards and sacred vessels. Among the administrative business at the time was the deprivation of three clergymen for unknown offences, the recantation of his heretical opinions by Richard Wytcombe of Holcombe, and the case of the new vicar of Locking in 1524 who was given three years to study when it was found on his appointment that he could not answer questions on the Seven Sacraments, the Articles of the Faith and the Seven Deadly Sins. Among some dubious appointments were several members of religious orders given parishes to care for and a young man under age made a prebendary of the cathedral.

Some of the appointments to parishes might raise a few questions today. Thomas Chard, prior of the Cluniac monastery of Montacute, was made vicar of Tintinhull in 1521; he was also a bishop, employed as suffragan both by Wolsey and Clerke, with the title of bishop of Solubria or Selymbria (now Silivri, west of Istanbul), and he needed an income to allow him to live as a bishop which the poverty of his cloister would not allow. Another suffragan, William Gilbert, was a native of Corton Denham, prior and abbot of Bruton, and bishop whose Latin title, *Majorensis*, has no modern equivalent but whose notional see was under the jurisdiction of the archbishop of Nazareth. He was also vicar of Minehead between 1507 and 1527 and of South Petherton probably until his death in 1535. A third bishop holding ordinations for Wolsey in the spring and summer of 1519 was Hugh Inge, bishop of Meath (and later archbishop of Dublin) who was probably staying at his family home in Shepton Mallet.

The bishop and his officers were not, of course, in ultimate control. Acts of Parliament and Royal Injunctions meant that they and clergy were answerable to the king in many ways, and when Henry VIII wanted to know how much the church might be worth (and thus worth tapping for much needed cash) he appointed a commission to discover just how much. The result was a

Nave Pulpit, Wells Cathedral, bearing the Arms of Bishop Knight, subsequently altered. Michael Blandford (© Dean & Chapter of Wells)

massive survey almost comparable to Domesday Book and known as the *Valor Ecclesiasticus*. It was compiled in 1535, the Bath and Wells part by a committee of Bishop Clerke, Sir William Stourton, Hugh Poulett, esquire (the bishop's chief steward), William Portman, gentleman, and Roger Kynsey, auditor. The bishop himself, they discovered, had a net income of £1843 4s 5d (£1843.22p) (more than the bishops of Salisbury or Exeter, a good deal less than Winchester or Durham), the cathedral as a corporate body £729 3s 4d (£729.16p), the dean himself £295 13s 1½d (£295.66p). Across the diocese there were huge differences. One of the richest parishes was Wraxall, where the rector received from his glebe farm, tithes of crops, wools and lambs, and offerings in church the huge total of £50 and his outgoings were only 8s 6d (42p), presumably because he served the chapels of Nailsea and Flax Bourton himself. The vicar of Chewton Mendip enjoyed a similar income but spent almost half in paying others to serve Emborough, Ston Easton, Farrington Gurney and Paulton. At the other end of the scale, and all in the Ile valley north of Ilminster, were South Bradon (£5 4s 2 ½d), Capland (£4 11s 7 ½d) and West Dowlish (£3 7s 6d) where the communities had shrunk, or Earnshill (£2 1s) and Goose Bradon (£1 6s 8d) from which people had entirely moved away and the only income was from the tithes of grazing land. (A decree by the bishop to extinguish South Bradon and unite it with Puckington in 1556 was completely ignored and the last rector, with no church and no people to care for, died in 1923).

As he valued the church's cash, so Henry VIII valued its prayers, and in the crisis years of the early 1540s prayers and processions were ordered on Wednesdays and Fridays; in 1543 for some ease from incessant rain, in 1544 for peace, and in 1545 for support for the king's navy against France and Spain. The church was thus harnessed for the nation; and more important, the prayers for the navy were to be sung in English. Just a few months later another order came, from the king himself through Archbishop Cranmer and from him to all bishops and clergy: a litany in English, described as 'a very good and godlye procession yn thinglish tongue' to be used on Sundays, workdays and festivals. An English bible, and now English prayers; a complete prayer book was not far away. Yet were prayers and bibles to be found in every church in the diocese, and were all the other orders and regulations being obeyed?

There is a good deal of evidence that, traditional or not, the church in the diocese was very much alive. During those crucial years from 1530 a least two churches, Bishop's Hull and Puxton, were almost entirely rebuilt, six new towers were put up, aisles added to make more room for processions and seats, windows to give more light and church houses to provide places for social gatherings were constructed in many places. Accounts of churchwardens tell of new seats, vestments, images and organs. The outward forms of worship were well supported by the worshippers in parish churches and chapels across the diocese. Bishops, through their archdeacons and courts, presumably heard and dealt with such complaints as were made, but that was still not enough for the king and in 1545 he appointed his faithful and most useful servant John Tregonwell

Puxton church, consecrated in 1540, had a rood loft and presumably screen. The loft was removed by sawing close to the wall and its imprint is seen behind the 17th-century pulpit. Robert Dunning

his vicar-general (a title Thomas Cromwell had held) to (according to the official phrase) reform the church by means of a series of enquiries in each diocese. His deputies in this diocese were the cathedral precentor George Dogeon and the lawyer John Daws. Dogeon and Daws discovered nothing to complain seriously about.

The findings of a second royal enquiry, in 1547, could not have proved happy reading for the reformers. Bibles were missing from ten churches and the clergy of Freshford and Queen Camel would not let their parishioners see their copies. Preaching was neglected and chancels, since the dissolution of the monasteries often the responsibility of laymen, were not repaired. There is hardly a trace of reformist attitudes: the wardens of St James's in Bath had allowed an image to be removed, and the parson of Stawley did not care for tapers on the altar 'but when they are lyghted by the clarke the person blowyth them owte agayne'. There is only one clear case of an extreme view: John Ligh of Kilmington (then in the diocese) was accused 'that in the tyme of procession with skornes [scorns] blesse[d] the font and toke the water in his hand and threw it in the faces of them that stode abowte him'.

PROTESTANTS IN CHARGE

No official record of the time William Barlow spent as bishop in the diocese between 1548 and 1553 has survived. That is a great pity, because the man who has been described as 'fanatical, iconoclastic, rash and often unscrupulous' as well as greedy, tactless and overbearing oversaw and no doubt personally influenced some revolutionary changes. His years at Wells were crucial to the Protestant Reformation in the county as a whole, covering the entire reign of Edward VI when men with radical ideas were in control.

Barlow was an Essex man, if not actually by birth certainly by calling. His early career offered no sign of his later outlook unless his amazing peregrinations between seven different religious houses in the area made him a little disappointed at not finding in them the secure and satisfying life of peace and prayer he might reasonably have expected. What is clear is that, having entered royal service, served as a diplomat and been rewarded with the headship of yet another priory, this time at Haverfordwest through the influence of Anne Boleyn, he became a fervent reformer. Clearly high in the favour of Thomas Cromwell, Barlow was part of a mission that tried (and failed) to persuade James V of Scotland to abandon the pope. His reward, even for failure, was to be appointed in quick succession, bishop of St Asaph and then of St David's.

The revolution of Edward VI's reign was carried out, like the radical changes of the later years of Henry VIII's reign, by Royal Injunction, Act of Parliament and the co-operation of the clergy meeting in convocation. Injunctions in 1547 were supposed to discourage the superstitious use of images and ceremonies and to encourage clergy to increase the amount of English used in church services. It was to be used especially in the epistle and gospel for the day, in one lesson each at matins and evensong, and in the litany, read at a desk rather than recited in processions. Acts of Parliament in that same year, 1547, declared that bread and wine, rather than bread alone, should be offered at communion to 'any person that will devoutly and humbly desire it'. Other Acts required that bishops were to be appointed directly by the king and that all chantries, colleges and free chapels should be handed over to the crown in exactly the same way that monasteries had been ten years earlier.

When radical theologians persuaded government that prayers for the dead were no longer necessary, then the end of chantries and their like was near. A national survey made in 1548 found that large and small endowments paid priests to say regular masses in special chapels inside or outside churches for long-dead founders and their families, and others for groups of parishioners who had clubbed together in a guild or brotherhood. Further funds provided lights before altars and images, and paid for prayers for individuals known as anniversaries or obits. In Somerset at the time there were at least 108 chantries, 32 free chapels, 4 hospitals or almshouses, 1 school (Crewkerne), 19 guilds, 1 college (North Cadbury) and 258 lights and obits that were considered to come within the meaning of an Act for their closure and sale. They were not, of course, as valu-

Chapel beside the south porch at Cheddar, perhaps housing one of the two chantries and one anniversary operating there in 1548. Robert Dunning

YOUR WORD IS A LAMP

able as the monasteries, but sales of pieces of ex-chantry property continued until James I's reign.

The foundations themselves varied a great deal in value and in their impact in a particular place. Some of the free chapels had already lost their original purpose - at Alstone Sutton in Lower Weare, Fodington in Babcary, in the churchyard at Congresbury and at Wiveliscombe and Winford they had either fallen down or were being used for storage, and the parishioners of Yatton were itching to demolish their chapel and use the stone to build a sluice gate on the moors. Some chapels clearly served a pastoral purpose like St Benignus's at Glastonbury or Catcott and their legal right to remain took much argument over several years. The chantry surveyors went even further at Langport, suggesting that since All Saints chapel was so near the parish church at Huish Episcopi (within a birdbolt shot, they said) it might reasonably be closed and sold. That decision was ultimately taken at the end of the twentieth century.

In comparison, the seven chantries and two guilds at St Mary's, Taunton, were still in working order, making the church a sort of religious community clearly lively enough to have recently seen through a huge rebuilding programme. The cathedral, naturally enough, had many more chantries and other similar operations whose priests were numerous enough to be gathered together in a college for mutual support.

Yet so far as the government was concerned, there was money to be made by closure, even though pensions had to be paid to the chantry chaplains, of whom in the diocese there were at least 87 including George Carew, hardly the most deserving case for he was not only chaplain of Trinity chapel or Whitehall in Ilchester but a royal chaplain, archdeacon of Totnes and a prebendary of both Exeter and Wells. In fact he was not even in the country at the time his pension was awarded but had gone abroad for five years to study 'languages, manners, men and good literature'. And not all was loss. A school at Ilminster, in addition to the one at Crewkerne, was guaranteed a future, for instance, and the rent paid up to 1548 by the corporation of Langport to the two brotherhood priests, one serving in the parish church, the other in the Hanging Chapel, was eventually remitted by the crown (as they had argued to the chantry surveyors) and went towards the maintenance of the Great Bridge.

▦ ▦ ▦

Much more revolutionary than the closure of the chantries was the first Act of Uniformity by which the nation's pattern of worship was laid down in a single, English, Luther-inspired and Cranmer-written prayer book. A second Act of Uniformity, passed in 1552, laid down penalties for not using a revised prayer book in which, for instance, the words 'mass' and 'altar' no longer appeared, showing how far Cranmer had moved from the doctrine of Real Presence (where the bread and wine became Christ's body and blood) to a communion of simple remembrance. The new book

The Prayer Books of 1549 and 1552. The rubric (instruction) in 1549 declares: The Priest beeyng in the quiet shall begynne with aloude voyce the Lordes prayer, called Paternoster. *In 1552 the rubric is more general:* The Mornyng and Evenyng praier shalbe used in such place of the Churche, Chapel or Chauncel, and the minister shall turne hyme, as the people may best here … and the chauncels shal remaine as they haue done in tymes paste. And here is to be noted that the Minister at the tyme of the communion, and at al other tymes of his ministracion, shall use neither Albe, Vestement, nor Cope: but beyng Archbishoppe, or Bishoppe, he shal haue and weare a rochet, and beyng a Prieste, or Deacon, he shal haue and weare a surplus onely. Michael Blandford. (© Dean and Chapter of Wells)

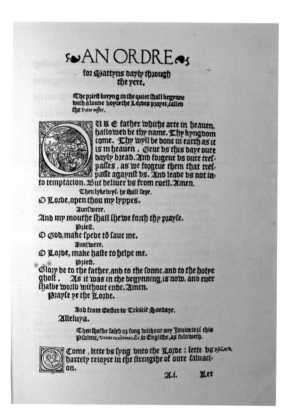
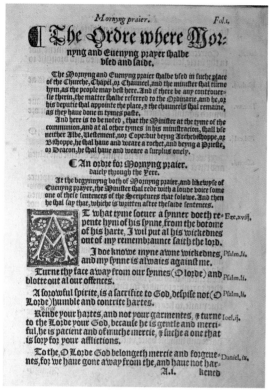

also permitted the priest or deacon to wear only a surplice and a bishop simply a rochet and entirely left out all prayers for the dead. One further, and very visible, change came about in 1550 following the lead of Bishop Ridley in London who had ordered the destruction of all altars (implying a sacrifice) and their replacement by simple, wooden tables.

It might be assumed that Bishop Barlow approved of all such measures and heartily supported their enforcement, but no official record of his actions has survived. His unpopularity in Wales, where he had proposed the removal of his cathedral from the traditional pilgrimage centre at St David's to Carmarthen and had given land and livings to his brothers, was evidently carried into Somerset where his bullying tactics could so easily make a bad impression and his fiery sermons a good one. The large estates attached to the bishopric certainly interested the rapacious Protector Somerset, virtual ruler of the land, and he demanded a large part of them including, for a time, his palace at Wells. The bullied bishop became bully himself and turned the dean out of his Deanery on a very flimsy excuse.

How far Barlow led and his clergy followed during his years at Wells is impossible to say,

The late-medieval velvet cope hidden under the pulpit at Othery for better times and now preserved at Glastonbury Abbey. Mathew Clements.

The screen and rood loft at Westonzoyland, a re-creation by W D Caroe, 1933-9. Robert Dunning

but one personal action was certainly significant. In December 1547 the clergy meeting in convocation approved of clerical marriage, a decision ratified by Parliament in 1549. Barlow himself took early advantage of the change, married a former nun, Agatha Welsborne, and by her had two sons and five daughters. Each of the daughters was to become the wife of a bishop. The bishop's example was followed by many Somerset clergy: Roger Lewis, vicar of Bedminster, John Hoskyns, rector of Charlcombe, John Smythe, rector of West Camel, and Thomas Locke, vicar of Ilminster and rector of Hatch Beauchamp all married in 1549 and many others obviously followed them. Locke was a former monk, probably of Muchelney.

As for the other radical measures, stone altars were removed and sometimes sold, roods (known as the Mary and John after the figures flanking the crucified Christ erected on rood screens, like the modern ones in the cathedral or at Westonzoyland) were taken down, images, mass vestments, service books and stained glass windows either hidden or disposed of. Still in 1557 the wardens of Lydeard St Lawrence noted that Simon Ven had a silver pyx (a box for holding consecrated wafers), Harry Mucchell had a chalice and the lead and iron from the Palm Cross and Richard Smyth five rings, leaving only one chalice for the parish. The cope found under the pulpit in Othery church and now displayed at Glastonbury Abbey was probably hidden in Bishop

Barlow's time in the hope of a return to the old ways. The people of Wick St Lawrence, in the full flow of reformist zeal, had painted texts from the Bible over walls formerly covered with images of saints like Christopher that served as visual aids for those who could not read. Victorian restorers often found pre-Reformation altar stones turned upside down and used as flooring.

REFORM REJECTED

The premature death of Edward VI and the failure of the plot to put Lady Jane Grey on the throne must have filled many people with foreboding, for Princess Mary had long been known as a traditionalist and the reform movement that had its political origin in her mother's annulment had obviously shaped her rigorous views. Bishop Barlow saw trouble coming and with John Taylor or Cardmaker, chancellor of the cathedral and vicar of Wellington, left by boat from Bristol presumably heading for some Protestant state on the continent. They were caught off the Cornish coast and had to appear before the Privy Council. Both were released and again tried to leave the country, and Barlow found himself in the Fleet prison in London. After two months he admitted that his radical opinions had been wrong, regained his freedom and promptly escaped abroad, finally settling in Poland. John Taylor was made of sterner stuff. His 78-year-old mother was examined in Wells by William Boureman, sub-dean of the cathedral on behalf of the new bishop, Gilbert Bourne, and told him that her son, himself a former Franciscan friar, had married a widow and that they had three children. Taylor was therefore deprived of his posts, and as his record as a fiery and radical preacher in London had not been forgotten he was closely examined. At first he agreed he had been wrong, but on second thoughts he stuck to his opinions and was burned as a heretic at Smithfield in 1555.

Dean William Turner and several cathedral canons, including the married George Carew, were removed in the next few months and then at a series of court sessions under Dr John Cottrell, the vicar-general, and William Boureman married clergymen were summoned, questioned, and deprived of their livings. They were then publicly humiliated by being required to take a vow of perpetual chastity while their former partners looked on, and then underwent public penance. The sight of clergymen 'bare footed, bare legged and bare headed' kneeling and holding a taper at mass, and declaring their misdemeanour aloud could have done nothing to dignify their former position in the eyes of many; and whether there were farewell feasts in their former parishes is not recorded. What is clear is that some refused to go through with such a charade and defied the bishop. Such was John Welshe, late vicar of Fivehead, who kept his wife and did not attend church. John More, late rector of West Monkton, was even more defiant: he was still 'conversant' with Joan 'his late pretended wife to whom he was late married' and the churchwardens reported 'that they will never depart [from each other] before their death'. Reginald Worthy, former rector of Marston Bigot, was duly deprived but he and his lady still lived together and three years later she, living in Frome, was reported as having 'had a child of late as she sayeth by her husband a priest which was parson of Marston'. He survived the wilderness and died as rector of Marston in 1576; what happened to his wife is not recorded. How many others slipped away quietly together we will never know.

What is certain, and proved harmful to the church in the diocese and probably much further afield, was that well over a hundred parishes and chapelries lost their priest and not much more than half were replaced quickly. Where were the rest to come from? The record of ordinations carried out by the suffragan bishop of Taunton, William Finch, between 1554 and 1559 suggests they came from almost anywhere but this diocese for the first two years and that the lack of ordinands caused something of a crisis. Candidates were rushed through two or more of the orders of acolyte, sub-deacon, deacon and priest in a few days, and William Seller managed to pass from acolyte to priest in six weeks. Among the candidates in September 1556 was William Absolom who was then made acolyte. In November he and William Good were given prebends in the cathedral, both conveniently vacant because the previous holders had been deprived. On that day the two were described as master and under-master of the 'grammar school lately set up' in the cathedral; a third vacant prebend was given to a pupil at the school 'on attaining the age of 12 years'. The school was clearly a training college for much-needed priests. In March 1557 seven of its pupils started on the road to priesthood by receiving the first tonsure, ten (including three already named) became acolytes, and one of those became also a sub-deacon. After that there was a steady trickle of candidates (though far fewer than the dozens of the 1490s) until Andrew Jeffries (first tonsure March 1557) was made deacon in March 1559. By the time he was priested in May he was vicar of North Petherton. He was one of only two products of the new grammar school to be given parishes in the diocese in Mary's reign, four more under Elizabeth. He soon lost it to the man who was vicar until 1554, came back in 1576 and remained until 1598.

The sudden loss of rector or vicar must have had profound personal and pastoral effects on parishes. The other changes demanded by the new government were liturgical. The stone altar, the rood, service books for the priest, vestments and lights must all be restored, and in addition a suitable and safe place to house the consecrated wafer - a demonstration of the real presence of God - to be secured first in a box suspended above the altar (known as a hanging pyx) and later in a small cupboard or tabernacle, in both cases safe from people prepared to make a mockery.

All those things, perhaps hidden away by traditionalists in the hope of better times or destroyed by radical enthusiasts, had to be replaced, but money was now not so easily found. Reports by churchwardens to the bishop tell their own tale. 'We have not our service according to the Queen's Law and also we have no altar and nothing for it', confessed the wardens of St Michael's, Bath. Two laymen had the alabaster altar and canopy that used to be in East Lydford church, and another man had kept and defaced the altar of Winscombe's Lady Chapel. Those

Hanging pyx, Wells Cathedral.
Michael Blandford (© Dean and Chapter of Wells)

Missal printed by Wynkyn de Worde in 1498, far more elaborate and expensive than those later available.

examples can be multiplied many times. At least thirty churches still had no 'Mary and John' in 1557, and St Cuthbert's at Wells had the perfect excuse. They had a crucifix only but 'dare not set up the same for fear of the steeple which is in decay'. And they were right: their tottery central tower came crashing down in 1561 and the screen that was evidently its main support must have been crushed.

In July 1554 at least 65 churches still lacked the vestments and ornaments that a few years earlier had been considered 'superfluous' and were now again essential for the proper celebration of mass. At Kilton there was no light before the altar and four images, once revered, had been sold by the parish clerk. At Bruton 'jewels and stuff' had been sold for £20 and resold for £28 and the wardens could not find the money to redeem them. Almost as many churches had no service books: Porlock 'not enough to celebrate divine service', Bathampton none at all 'nor as yet can get none but that be borrowed'. The parson of Combe Hay, deliberately or out of sheer necessity, 'reads the homilies [prepared sermons] and procession in the English tongue for lack of a Latin book'. Combe Florey lacked a chalice, a cope, a mass book, processional, antiphoner and holy water bucket.

The replacement of such things was costly. A new stone altar at Yatton cost 12s 4d (62p), a processional, missal (mass-book) and manual (book of rituals) together 25s 2d (£1.26p) and finding them a further 7d (3p), a portas (small book of daily prayers) 20s (£1) and a tabernacle 26s 8d (£1.33p). Yatton could afford the cost but at St Michael's in Bath the wardens spent 2s 10d (14p) on a manual but had to buy vestments by instalments. Emborough was in a worse state. The wardens admitted in 1557 that they had no rood and no tabernacle and their building programme had come to a standstill because all their funds had gone on timber.

The contradictory teaching that had emerged since the 1530s produced confusion in the minds of many and cynicism among a few. The devout were disturbed and those for whom any kind of imposed belief was unacceptable had an opportunity to display their objections. Mystery had for some become no better than magic, and the numinous had been somehow destroyed by government decree. 'There stay priest, thou sayest not well', shouted Hugh Simson of Hinton St George when the curate of Crewkerne was preaching on the mass; and Isabel Jenyngs, a farm servant from Cameley would not reverently hold up her hands and kneel down when the priest raised the consecrated wafer. Joan Rowberye of Othery 'will not come to church to hear God's divine service being warned of it; and when she cometh to church she sitteth in the porch and turneth her tayle toward the sacrament'. A group of twenty-six people from Chewstoke 'do not regard the mass and also despise with holy bread and holy water and with the sacrament of the altar'; and one man from the same parish 'reported openly that a dog may confirm children as well as my lord bishop'. Christopher Clement from Downhead was even more outspoken: his hand was as good to deliver the sacrament as any priest's, his hand was better than a sheep skin to handle the chalice and 'his mare will make as good holy water as any priest can'. Here were the socially humble and uneducated expressing crudely and graphically some of the teaching of the reformers: the spiritual had somehow disappeared.

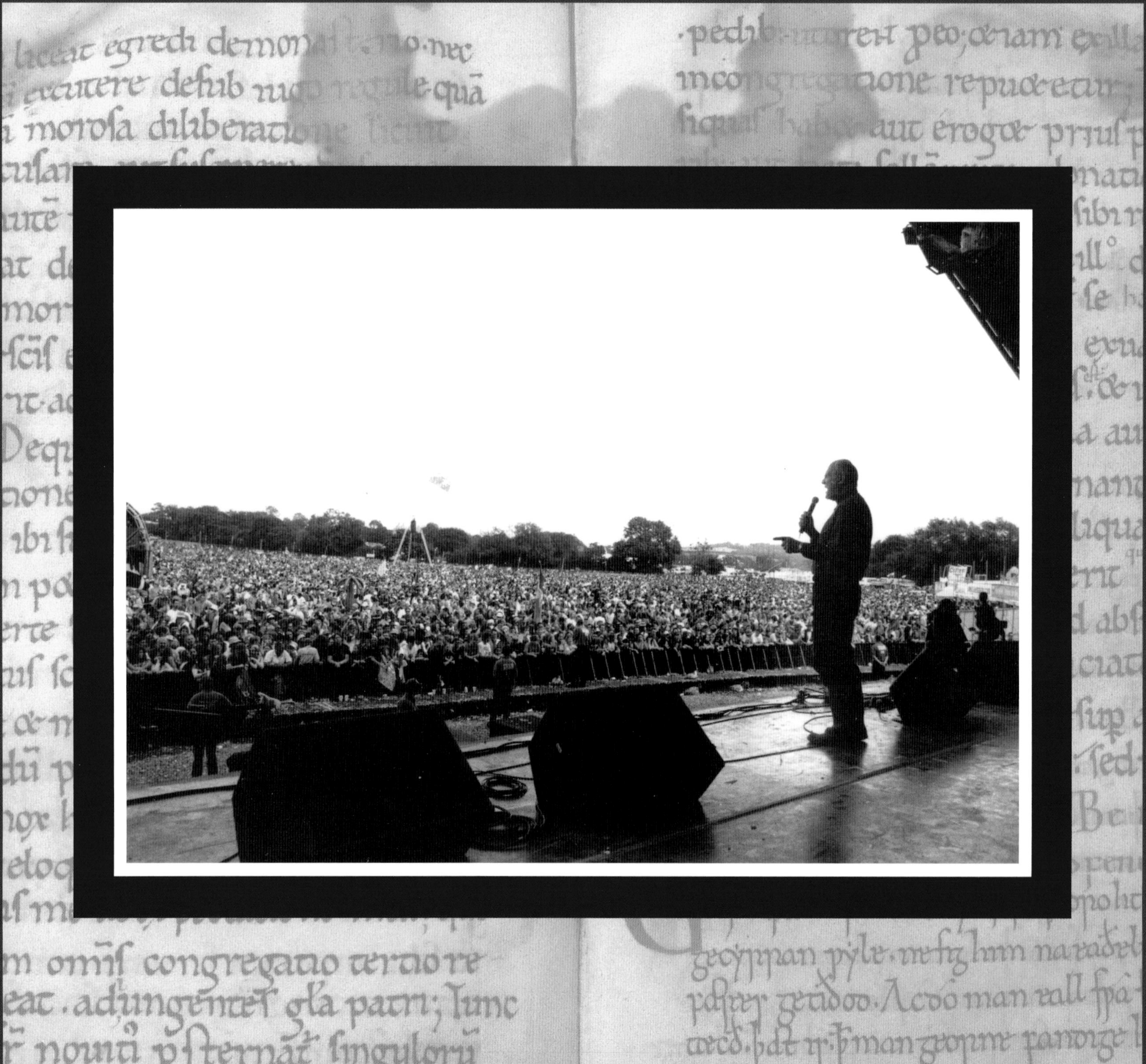

7

If God is for Us

Rom. 8. 31

There was no doubt at all that when the ailing Queen Mary died her sister Princess Elizabeth would bring more changes to the Church of England. Too many people had suffered torture or death, though perhaps only four in Somerset; and what emerged was a compromise with few reprisals. It was a compromise imposed by law and the will of the monarch rather than the result of any democratic process, and at various times during the next eighty years differing views seemed to gain the upper hand depending on the personal intervention of the monarch and of those church leaders the sovereign had appointed. External events were also important, notably the invasion attempt by Spain, the excommunication of Elizabeth by the pope, and the Gunpowder Plot, all putting catholic loyalists under deep suspicion of treason for the faith they held on purely religious grounds.

The essential argument within the church lay in the freedom given by Henry VIII to interpret the Bible, a consequence that would have horrified the king. The lamp of the word led the feet of some into paths suggesting that the headship of the church lay with God and his clergy, for in the scriptures they could find no bishop, no archdeacon, no cathedral, no elaborate ceremonial. The 'sovereignty of the Word of God' led them instead to self-regulating groups of like-minded clergy meeting, preaching and praying together (prophesyings or exercises they were called) or, in more extreme versions, independent groups of laymen and women employing ministers as their pastors. Thus were Presbyterians and Congregationalists born.

Such ideas struck at the power of the crown and the establishment. Queen Elizabeth saw bishops as her creatures, their wealth worth whittling down to keep them subservient, their wives thoroughly disapproved of, but providing stirring sermons when she was willing to listen and still the only way to deal with religious extremists. For James and Charles the useful ones were those who supported the high royal view and found the court and government a worthy field of

Opposite page:
If God is for us. Phil Day 2004 (© Templar Trust)

83

The Arms of James I have taken the place of the figures of the rood above the screen at Croscombe.
Robert Dunning

endeavour, just like their medieval predecessors. Ultimately they subscribed to the royal slogan: no bishop, no king. Yet when a particularly outspoken subscriber to that view, the young William Laud, preached a sermon in support of bishops, taking as his theme the 'perpetual continuity of the true church', Archbishop Abbot of Canterbury was infuriated by such lack of tact; for compromise continued to be the goal in the conference at Hampton Court that achieved a measure of agreement between the parties, the Canons of 1604, and in the great scheme of biblical translation that resulted in the King James Bible, the Authorised Version. The ultimate failure of that compromise was an important contributory factor in the political and social division that led to civil war.

'THAT HIGH HONOUR AND CALLING'

That phrase used by Leonard Mawe when declaring himself to be unworthy to be bishop of Bath and Wells in 1628 might also have been used by Bishop Bourne, in many ways the last of the medieval bishops of the diocese and certainly the last traditionalist until William Laud in 1626. Bourne had served Queen Mary loyally but the first parliament of Queen Elizabeth repealed her sister's laws and the bishops were required to take an oath of loyalty to the new queen as Supreme Governor. That they could hardly do, but Gilbert Bourne, hiding in his manor house at Wiveliscombe, was one of the last to refuse and was imprisoned with his fellow bishops in the Tower of London. He was released in 1561, first under the supervision of his friend George Carew, dean of Bristol, archdeacon of Exeter and dean of the queen's chapel, in whose church at Silverton he was buried in 1569. William Finch, suffragan bishop of Taunton since 1538, was probably saved by death from similar exile.

There followed as the new bishop, with necessary speed, an almost exact contemporary of Bourne in the person of Gilbert Berkeley whose clerical career had begun in Northampton as a Franciscan friar but who, through his (socially unacceptable) marriage and his protestant opinions, had gone into exile in Frankfurt in Queen Mary's reign but who had returned to become a royal chaplain. Someone who knew him but did not care for bishops admitted he was a 'good justicer' (whatever that meant); he once expressed himself in favour 'of prophesyings' on the grounds that they at least might help to raise clerical standards. He was also keen that clergy should follow the rules of dress as required by the Book of Common Prayer, but his attempt to insist on the matter where Dean William Turner was concerned caused an unseemly confrontation.

Berkeley's principal concern was his poverty, making the hospitality expected of a bishop impossible. The estates of the see, depleted under Bishop Barlow, had been diminished still further by Bourne. Banwell, Westbury and Wiveliscombe passed on favourable leases to his brother and nephews (the brother also ran the administration of all the estates) and Berkeley's only remaining home, the palace at Wells, was in a dreadful state, parts let to unsuitable tenants. Given his chronic sciatica, he found the palace with its 'low' site and 'cold air' 'not very wholesome'. That added to his general depression and a belief that with a net income of much less than £1000 he could hardly carry out the task expected of him. Some thought him 'lax' in his administration of the see and he died of a 'lethargy' in November 1581 at the age of 80.

Thomas Godwin, whose family motto was 'Win God Win All', came to Wells as an ageing widower suffering from quartan ague and gout and encumbered with five sons and three daughters. Such were the standards of the times that there followed an unseemly scramble for offices and places so successful that a son-in-law administered the courts of the bishop's estates until 1596 and one son succeeded another in a cathedral stall and survived until turned out when the cathedral establishment was abolished in 1643. Bishop Godwin's innate good nature did his family proud. In his youth either his radical views or his marriage lost him his college fellowship at Oxford and perhaps his domestic situation inclined him to choose a new career (medicine) rather than exile under Queen Mary. Queen Elizabeth found him a most acceptable preacher though he

Thomas Godwin (bishop 1584-90), copy 1827 of original in Christchurch, Oxford, artist unknown. Bishop's Palace, Wells

had been outspoken in support of reform of the prayer book services and had insisted that the Word of God should take precedence over church tradition on the question of vestments. He may thus have given some comfort to the radicals of the diocese. Under him, however, the bishop's income was reduced still further: he successfully defended his right to Banwell against Sir Walter Raleigh who coveted it, but he was forced to give a 99-year lease of his largest estate, Wiveliscombe, to the Crown. He died in 1590.

The 'Divine Still' came to Wells in 1593 after another long vacancy, learned, wise, an excellent preacher and particularly good in disputations. Most of his career had been spent at Cambridge or at his home at Hadleigh in Suffolk with a wife and nine children. One of his pupils at Cambridge described him remarkably as one 'to whom I never came but I grew more religious; from whom I never went but I parted better instructed'. His was a steady hand in the years of crisis when MPs called for the end of the sort of greed shown by the Godwins, the closure of cathedrals and a radical revision of the prayer book. He is to be remembered for the business-like way he exploited the Mendip lead mines for the benefit of the see.

Less than a month after John Still died, James Montague was nominated to the see. Successively dean of Lichfield and Worcester and also dean of the royal chapel, he was by birth an aristocrat. He was also the first master of the puritan Sidney Sussex college, Cambridge, but also the dreadfully obsequious editor of King James's Collected Works. He left the king a valuable gold cup in recognition of 'high favours' done to him, clearly a courtier bishop. Montague was personally generous, thanks to the good works done by Bishop Still on the Mendip mines and his most famous gift was the sum to complete the roofless Bath Abbey. At his death he wished to be buried there in a prominent spot 'to stir up more benefactors to that place'. Montague was translated from Wells to Winchester in 1616 and died two years later. Perhaps a more significant memorial is the part he played in the translation of the King James Bible.

Arthur Lake, bishop 1616-26, was also a man with royal connections but also of very wide interests ranging from Arabic to geography and music. His was a moderate, calming influence over the contending voices to be heard in the diocese where, he observed, controversy among leaders led to division within parishes. He personally carried out three visitations of the diocese, established a public library at Bath Abbey to encourage local clergy in their preaching, and himself preached sermons (99 were printed in one volume with 11 meditations) ranging from formal cathedral discourses to homilies when people did public penance. But for his age, he told the settler-leader John White, he would have gone with him to convert the people of the New World.

For less than two years after Lake's death the diocese was held by a man in a hurry. William Laud's belief that the Church of England was true heir to the pre-Reformation church in both doctrine and practice had brought him great trouble at Oxford in his youth, when to be seen in his company was tantamount to heresy. His passion for his cause brought him martyrdom and the

Pulpit in Croscombe church dated 1616 and bearing the Arms of Bishop Lake and the text: Blessed are they that heare the word of God and keepe it. *Probably ordered at the bishop's visitation.*
Robert Dunning

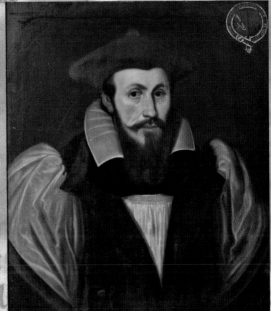

Clockwise from top left:

John Still (bishop 1593-1608), after original in Trinity college, Cambridge. Bishop's Palace, Wells

James Montague (bishop of Bath and Wells 1608-16) (label incorrect), artist unknown. Bishop's Palace, Wells

Walter Curll (bishop of Bath and Wells 1629-32), as bishop of Winchester 1635, artist unknown. Bishop's Palace, Wells

Arthur Lake (bishop 1616-26), by John Payne, 1628. Bishop's Palace, Wells

church he championed short-term destruction, but in the 1620s and 1630s his was the voice that Charles I wanted to hear. It was a voice that none heard in person in the diocese; he had visited the see of St David's twice when its bishop; Wells never saw him at all.

Leonard Mawe, Laud's successor, was so reluctant to leave Cambridge that death overtook him on the way before he reached further than Chiswick where he died in 1629. He was followed by another worthy Cambridge man, Walter Curll. He had been a long-time royal chaplain and for a short time (July 1628-Sept 1629) holder of the very poor see of Rochester. Almost three years later Curll was translated to Winchester and William Piers, bishop of Peterborough, took his place.

Piers was an Oxford man both by birth and education, and businessman rather than cleric but with very strong views on the high position of the church. He was clearly a follower of the doctrines of Laud and where most of his predecessors had strong personal views that were generally moderated by circumstance, Piers was quite unable to see that strict enforcement of the law was not always the wisest course. His demands that church ales, hated by puritans, should be continued or revived, that afternoon lectures (usually delivered by puritan ministers) should cease and that communion tables should be placed at the east end of the church and be suitably railed were not easily enforced and his reports to Laud that all was well were either figments of his imagination or deliberate evasions. Yet Piers, who must be held personally responsible for some of the local divisions of the church in the diocese, lived, like King Charles, to return and enjoy his own again.

THE BISHOPS' OFFICIALS

The importance of administrative officials in the government of the medieval church is reflected in frequent references to them in the records they created, but such references in the post-Reformation period are both fewer and somewhat less seemly. Bishop Berkeley complained about the registrar, William Lancaster, the official keeper of the records of the diocese and a lawyer, as 'a manifest enemy to God and the queen's majesty'. He had certainly been a friend of Bishop Bourne and probably a traditionalist in his religious views. He held the office jointly with another lawyer, Richard Snow. Berkeley was somehow persuaded to change his opinion and some time later he confirmed the office to Lancaster, his son Roger and John Bishop. In 1587 Bishop Godwin decided instead to appoint Robert Owen and two others, whose names happened to be Godwin, though not perhaps relatives. Owen agreed to pay Lancaster £52 a year in compensation after his appointment in 1588 and began to question the activities of the registrars of the archdeacons. Perhaps he subsequently learnt his lesson, for when in 1598 Edward Huishe became the bishop's registrar, he was warned not to interfere with the work of the registrars of the dean, the dean and chapter, the three archdeacons, the sub-dean or any of the prebendaries on pain of forfeiture of a bond of £133 6s 8d (£133.32p). The fees lawyers took for church business were evidently worth fighting for.

The office of bishop's chancellor was potentially more important for the holder was usually also vicar-general and thus head of the bishop's consistory court. During this period, interestingly, he was not also a member of the cathedral chapter, perhaps because the study of church law had been dropped by would-be clergy. The chancellor Bishop Still inherited when he came in 1593 was Dr Gilbert Bourne, a lawyer-nephew of the former bishop who had also been receiver-general of the estates of the see since his boyhood in 1555. Dr Bourne died during the course of Bishop Still's primary visitation during which the bishop had himself been present for the first main court for each deanery and a total of 26 times out of a total of 132 sittings. Otherwise Dr Bourne had been the sole judge until illness forced him to appoint deputies (surrogates), all of them clergymen. Dr Francis James, another lay lawyer, succeeded him in 1596. James was succeeded in 1616 by Dr Arthur Duck, whose close friendship both with Bishop Lake, archdeacons Timothy Revett of Bath and Samuel Ward of Taunton and, from his appointment in 1621, with Dean Ralph Barlow, created a most effective and unusual administrative force. Bishop William Piers perhaps tried to replicate the amazing notion of cooperation when he appointed his son William to be archdeacon to succeed Revett in 1638 and to succeed Ward in 1643. Dr Duck was still the chancellor.

The courts that the registrars administered and the chancellors presided over followed the same procedures to enforce the same law as the courts of pre-Reformation England. Bishop Piers evidently noticed a certain laxity when the names of the rural deans from the archdeaconry of Taunton were not returned and his experience in his attempts to bring churchwardens to heel, notably in the Beckington case, demonstrated for the whole country how weak was the law of the church and its means of enforcement in the face of civil disobedience.

NEW RADICALS AND NEW CONSERVATIVES

There were no such wholesale and damaging removals of Somerset clergy in 1559-60 as had taken place in 1554. Several of the cathedral canons were removed over the next few years including John FitzJames, archdeacon of Taunton, some because of their theological views, some for persistent absence. Parish clergy of differing views were in some cases restored to parishes they had lost in 1554, others were left alone; pastoral care seems to have been more important than doctrinaire policy, and the supply of even adequate clergy was a critical issue. Just as William Boureman and John Cottrell, Bishop Bourne's chief officers, remained as canons in the cathedral, so most of the parish clergy remained at first unchanged, at least until their reactions to the new Acts of Parliament and Royal Injunctions were worked out or until suitable replacements could be found. The new regulations were certainly a compromise. They involved yet another version of public worship, very much like the second Prayer Book of Edward VI but permitting other vestments besides the surplice at certain times and including in the words of administration at communion both 'The body of Christ ...' and 'Do this in remembrance ...' which brought the doctrines of the Real Presence and a commemorative meal together. Royal Injunctions permitted bishops and clergy to marry with defined approval and (another compromise) required the removal of stone altars and other objects associated with the mass, replacing them with holy tables to stand where altars had stood against the east wall of the chancel, but which could be moved for communion services to places 'whereby the minister may be more conveniently heard'.

The most radical of the clergy as a whole, later to be called puritans and in the 1560s very strong in Convocation, lost by just one vote a series of proposals which would have abandoned most feast days, insisted that the priest faced the people at communion, that a 'comely garment' and square cap would be the alternative to the surplice, that the sign of the cross be not used at baptism, and left to each bishop's discretion whether the people knelt or stood to receive communion. The question of priestly vestments would not go away until the puritans went further, suggesting the priest should be chosen by popular election and bishops be altogether abolished. Government should be by synod, that is, by meetings of clergy in presbyteries. Those clergy also met together to study and expound the Bible, showing off their undoubted learning before a few invited laity. Those 'prophesyings' had the merit of encouraging many ignorant clergy to improve themselves, but the queen did not care for such underhand behaviour and banned them.

In another camp were those few who still looked to the pope as head of the church. There had been a good deal of tolerance of such folk, but the action of the pope in 1570 in excommunicating the queen and any who supported her effectively meant that every catholic from that time was a Roman Catholic and a traitor and should bear the consequences. The 'invasion' of the country by Jesuit missionaries from 1580 (including John Hambley, arrested at Chard and condemned to death at Taunton and Robert Persons, born at Nether Stowey and executed in London) meant that the few families refusing to attend their parish church (hence popish recusants) were faced with the full rigour of the law and paid fines of £20 a month.

Uniformity was what the law and most of the bishops required, and those people who did not conform were in varying amounts of trouble, depending on the inclinations or energies of the bishop and the efficiency and temper of his officers. Uniformity, perhaps the result of puritan pressure, required in 1572 that chalices once used for the mass be melted down and turned into cups for communion; and it was so, if the number of vessels dated 1573-4 is any guide, compared with the very few chalices, such as those from Nettlecombe and Chewton Mendip, that were saved. The wardens of Trull made a notional profit of 7s 2d (36p) on the transaction, because the new cup was lighter than the old chalice. Most people seem already to have accepted communion as a meal, taken around the holy table with the cup passing from hand to hand among the communicants.

In the 1570s, perhaps a third of the parishes of the diocese were in the care of ill-paid and probably ill-trained curates who came and went in bewildering succession. Buckland Dinham had a vicar who stayed for a year and then 'they did hire curates by the month and by the week as they might get them'. Marksbury's churchwardens looked back to the time when Richard Hadleye had been resident rector in Queen Mary's time. He had gone when Elizabeth became queen, making way for William Jennysone who had been removed as a married priest in 1554. He stayed until his death but for ten years they had nothing but curates. Both Kingston Seymour and Broomfield had French priests, but the one at Broomfield stayed only three months and 'upon the soden departed'; the £8 promised for the year was not enough to live on.

Creech St Michael was as well off as any parish at the time for David Marler had been serving there for ten years; but his predecessor John Bullingham, now elevated to be archdeacon of Huntingdon and even later bishop of Gloucester and Bristol, had preferred to serve for three years as the preacher employed by the corporation of Bridgwater, leaving Creech to the care of curates.

When the bishop and his archdeacons went on their visitations they heard complaints from clergy and laity alike. In 1576 among the parishes around Taunton the parson at Bagborough was away studying at Oxford, the vicar of St Mary's, Taunton, had two churches; the required quarterly sermons had not been preached at all at Stoke St Mary, Ruishton and Wilton, and only twice in the year at Bishop's Hull; the rector of Cheddon kept a woman in his house whom he claimed was a relative, and the curate there was suspected of having no licence from the bishop to officiate. But it was the people who were the greater backsliders - one or two absentees from church in nearly every parish, an illiterate parish clerk at Bagborough, a woman from Ash Priors suspected of being a papist because she gave an old woman 1d to pray for her husband's soul; and Robert Sealie of North Curry who behaved irreverently in church, talking and not taking his hat off at the name of Jesus.

Twenty years on and the wardens of Bishop's Hull were concerned that their Bible dating from Edward VI's time might not be 'sufficient' and reported (incorrectly as it turned out) that the schoolmaster at Taunton castle did not attend his parish church. The parson at West Monkton was absent, the people of Stoke still had no sermons, and the cover of the communion cup was missing at Cothelstone. But there was clearly real trouble at St Mary's, Taunton. Parishioners were said to be 'very negligent' in not sending their children to be taught the faith, two people were thought to be recusants and they and another had been very rude to the vicar. Worst of all, well over 200 named people had not received communion at Easter or stood excommunicated. Already the county's largest manufacturing town was displaying its strong rebellious tendency. There were no such problems at Bath: just two people not at Easter communion in the whole of the city and the worst record at St Michael outside the North gate where there had been no quarterly sermons and no catechising, and where two of the congregation came once a month. But not far away was what became a familiar story: Evan Thomas, vicar of South Stoke, would not wear a surplice nor use the sign of the cross in baptism, he ignored parts of the prayer book to make room for two sermons each Sunday, and would not celebrate communion until the whole parish understood its meaning.

Those reports from the Taunton area and Bath were exactly the sorts of things that churchwardens across the diocese reported to bishops and archdeacons. And visitations were expensive affairs. In 1594 Somerton wardens paid out a total of 10s 8d (56p) in fees and other expenses, for they and four sidesmen had to travel to Wells, there to report that William Odams was teaching without the bishop's licence, that Peter Hurd and his wife were not living together and that Peter Guppy, James Hayward and Elizabeth Harris were all excommunicated and had done nothing to return to the fold of the church.

Those same wardens and many like them, no longer received gifts to be spent on prayers for the dead, to maintain chapels and images, to provide candles for the rood or the Easter Sepulchre, to find vestments for the colourful celebration of the mass at different festivals. Instead their income was usually from a regular rate imposed on all parishioners, the sale of seats and payments for ringing the knell at funerals. Their main spending was on bells and bell ropes, repairs (but hardly any new building), washing the surplice, visitation fees, wages of the parish clerk and sexton, and bread and wine for quarterly communions.

THE WORD AUTHORISED

King James I fancied himself as a theologian and it was his earnest wish, after his troubles in Scotland, to bring together the opposing factions that divided the church in England. The arguments between puritan clergy and traditionalists were unchanged: was religion a mystery where ceremony and ritual were essential in approaching God; or was it rather, what emerged from learned treatises especially on pastoral subjects, that preaching and therefore listening to sermons was the main activity of clergy and people?

From the meeting between the divided leaders at Hampton Court in 1604 there finally emerged from futile debate the request for a new translation of the Bible. The request had come from a puritan leader, the acceptance came from the king. The new translation, to be made by the best scholars of every persuasion working together, would, unlike the Geneva Bible which the puritans so loved for its anti-royalist notes, and the various other translations, be generally acceptable for all, 'reviewed' by the bishops, 'presented' to the Privy Council and 'ratified' by royal authority. It was to be the Bible to be read in churches to the exclusion of all others. It was not at all what the puritans wanted, but it was what they came to accept. It was, so it turned out, surprisingly conservative in expression, but its contribution to our language and literature, let alone to our understanding of our faith, was and remains profound.

There were at least fifty translators, arranged in 'companies', and the most significant was the Second Oxford Company charged with the Gospels, the Acts of the Apostles and the Book of

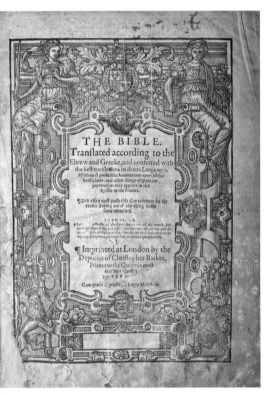

Geneva Bible, 1560. Michael Blandford (© Dean and Chapter of Wells)

the Revelation of St John. Perhaps the strongest and most powerful member of that company was James Montague, dean of the king's chapel and soon to be bishop of Bath and Wells. Its Director was Thomas Ravis, bishop of Gloucester, and another member was the gloomy George Abbot, later archbishop of Canterbury. Montague's theology was puritan but his instincts were political and royalist; his precise role as Translator is unknown.

Another Translator, eventually with Somerset connections, was a member of the Second Cambridge Company, responsible for the Apocrypha. He was Samuel Ward, another puritan and a Cambridge friend of Montague, whose diary reveals a man for ever struggling with his conscience - plums were his passion and over-eating his weakness. He was Montague's first chaplain from 1606 and collected from the bishop the vicarage of Yatton, the archdeaconry of Taunton (he failed to get the archdeaconry of Bath earlier) and a house in the cathedral close. He remained archdeacon until his death in 1643; his proudest achievement, he believed, was to have been a Translator.

The work of Montague, Ward and the rest was submitted to a committee of two from each company who, adding chapter summaries, a Dedication to the king and a long Preface, somehow brought a unity to the whole enterprise. It was a puritan text, carefully changed here and there

Far left: *The Authorised Version, 1611.*

Left: *Title page of the 1632/3 edition of the Authorised Version, once owned by Robert Creighton (dean 1660-70, bishop 1670-2)* Michael Blandford (© Dean and Chapter of Wells)

Below: *The Lord's Prayer, Authorised Version, Catcott.* Robert Dunning

by men with a wider vision able to accept that an original word in one context might be translated differently in another and a passion for clarity over obscurity. Bishop Smith's Preface, sadly now seldom read, was the work of one who had no love for a catholic past but took his place firmly beside the protestant leaders of the Reformation, convinced that the Bible came from heaven, not earth; that its author was God, not man; that its writer was the Holy Spirit, not the wit of Apostles and Prophets. And in clear and beautiful English it was an acceptable text for the church, authorised to be read in churches to the exclusion of all others.

At Bishop Still's visitation in 1606 the churchwardens of Wilton presented that their curate had conducted marriages at unlawful times (including mid-night), had baptised an illegitimate child from another parish and was suspected of not having the bishop's license to serve. A parishioner remained excommunicated. The curate fled rather than face court proceedings. Somerset Record Office D/D/Va 151.

A CHURCH BY ROYAL ORDER

Both James I and Charles I took their position as Supreme Governor very seriously and they expected their bishops to support their views. William Piers, an ardent disciple of William Laud, put the full authority of his office at the king's disposal, never realising either the strength of opposition, both from clergy and lay people, to his 'high church' views, or the ineffectiveness of his powers of coercion. He might, and certainly did, hold visitations in an attempt to root out all who were not following his orders, but the very repetition of those orders is an indication that they had no effect.

The answers given by churchwardens to his questions in 1634 fall into three main groups. First, the church houses where a century and more ago church ales had been held to raise money for building or other expenses, had been abandoned under puritan pressure or put to other uses: 'decayed and ruinated' at Blagdon, shared between school and poorhouse at Ditcheat, a poorhouse only at Cucklington, 'defective in windows, flooring and other necessaries' at Chewton Mendip, taken by the parson and allowed to decay at Walton, needing a new loft at Compton Bishop. Yet, given support, some church houses and ales continued a while longer: Williton chapel wardens held ales regularly until 1628, again in 1636 and from 1639-41; and revived them in 1663 and continued them until 1689.

Church house and ale had been at the centre of those revels that in earlier days had marked the dedication feast of every church and had often, with the bishop's permission, been transferred to Sundays without criticism. Now those revels by royal command were to be revived by the publication in church of the King's Book of Sports, and Bishop Piers ordered the book to be read from every pulpit: his second point of attack on puritans.

Yet here for many clergy was Sabbath breaking by order of the king and sanction of the bishop. George Newton, vicar of St Mary's, Taunton, read instead Exodus 20.8 (Remember the Sabbath Day to keep it holy) and told his congregation to choose between God and man. Clearly he and those who thought like him had a point. Thomas Aplegate of Shepton Mallet said 'that all those that goe to Revells are Rebells ... contrarie to the lawes of God', and innocent games led to others less worthy: fives against the church towers at Binegar, Mells, Compton Dundon and many others including Mudford where damage had been caused to nearby windows. Timing of the games was crucial - by law after church service, not before, but at St Cuthbert's in Wells there was 'hewering and trimereinge' of a maypole while the bell tolled for morning prayer and the process involved a drum and other instruments. The wardens of South Barrow reported bowls playing at the wrong time, there was cudgel playing between morning and evening prayer at Bridgwater, and much disturbance at North Cadbury when during morning prayer and sermon a company from Galhampton and elsewhere 'with a morrice daunce and with fidlers and with a drume ... held on theire sports so neere unto the Church' and refused to stop though the parson twice asked them 'to leafe makeinge such a noyse'. Sports in some places were amazingly varied. The vicar of Chew Magna, claiming possession of a field beside the church at Dundry, went through the whole gamut: a maypole, dancing, sporting, kissing, bull baiting, cocking, bowling, shooting at butts, cudgel playing, tennis playing 'and divers others sports and plays'. The field was also the site of the annual St Giles fair and fives were played against the church tower. Merrie England at its merriest.

Bishop Piers' third issue was the position of the communion table in church. It seems that between a quarter and a third of his clergy defied their bishop and refused to move the table back to the east wall from the centre of the chancel, and the response was particularly bad in the north-east of the diocese. There were, of course, some practical excuses: the workman making the rails for Shapwick had not yet turned up, and the table at Wolverton had been turned to the required east-west position but was not railed. George Jones of Mells, however, had brought the table to the lower end of the chancel and was going to continue to celebrate from there. The notorious churchwardens of Beckington long defied the bishop over the same question.

The true Portraiture of the Learned Mʳ William Sclater D D

William Sclater, vicar of Pitminster, prosecuted for nonconformity in 1606, was approved of by Bishop Lake, who made him a prebendary of the cathedral in 1616. Somerset Archaeological Society

The nave ceiling, Axbridge, 1636.
John Page

When the bishop's court heard a dispute about ownership of the north aisle of West Buckland church in 1606 it was neither the first nor the last of its kind. Pews, aisles and chapels had become pieces of real property to be bought, sold and squabbled over. What makes the case of interest is the evidence of a few witnesses with long memories. One of those men recalled some memorial glass in a window depicting two figures with an inscription beginning ORATE, signifying donors asking for prayers for their souls; another remembered that an altar had stood in the aisle, another an augmented group of singers at funerals and another that as a boy of twelve he took the Pax (a tablet of perhaps precious metal with a depiction of the Crucifixion) around the congregation to be kissed. The mass and its accompanying liturgy were gone; a distant memory perhaps regretted, perhaps not. The aisle had instead become a place for a local gentleman to display his social and economic status.

The inspiration had somehow gone from worship, the imagination suppressed. The arches of Batcombe church were considered in the 1630s to be painted in colours 'too light and wanton' and order was given 'to make the same over with more grave and civil colours better fitting a church'. The ceilings at Axbridge and East Brent offered a different and rarer view, but the fall of Keynsham's spire during a tempest in 1632 that destroyed the rest of the building pointed to the problem the puritans had created for themselves. The wardens were forced to resort to an appeal for funds across southern England because the people of the parish were 'men of small ability [to pay] ... for the most part ... poore handicrafts men'. Had church ales not been suppressed, those poor men and their wives would have raised the money; in the event rebuilding only came to an end when the weathercock was placed on the tower in 1655.

By then Keynsham folk had been caught up in civil war and revolutionary governments that followed. They would have been affected in some way by the demands of the Crown for Ship Money, a tax imposed in the absence of a parliament allegedly for the defence of the realm against invasion. For more money when troops were needed to enforce the king's church policy in Scotland, Charles I turned to the English church. Bishop Piers, Dean Barlow, the archdeacons of Wells and Taunton and the parson of Wrington between them promised six fully equipped lancers, 12 parish clergy including the rectors of West Monkton, High Ham, Lympsham and Chiselborough 10 light horsemen, the chancellor, precentor and sub-dean of the cathedral, the rectors of Wraxall and Winford and the vicar of Chew Magna with others promised 11 petronells (carbines for horsemen) and other clergy through deaneries 223 muskets and 9 corslets (sets of body armour). Frome deanery produced the largest contribution with 30 muskets, Bedminster deanery 24 muskets and 2 corslets, Bath 11 muskets. It was not a voluntary contribution but one based on the estimated income of each living, hence a note that Keynsham had somehow not been charged though it was worth £40, that the contributions from Norton Malreward and Tickenham might be halved and that of Ubley increased. The involvement of church leaders in raising troops and armaments for an operation in Scotland was but a short step, and in a very short time, to being parties in a civil war at home.

Richard Bernard, 'most vigilant' vicar of Batcombe 1613–42. Portrait by Wenceslaus Hollar 1641. Somerset Archaeological Society

NO ALCOHOL
NO SMOKING
We welcome you
Please
Respect others
Respect the space
Enjoy your stay

8

Not Dead But Sleeping

Matthew 9.24

Charles I and Archbishop Laud eventually failed in their attempt to impose their high church views and Bishop Piers was obliged to face the truth that many clergy and leading laymen were more independent-minded and even radical than he cared to believe. In 1641 over 14,000 Somerset folk declared themselves in favour of bishops among whom 221 were clergy, and the remainder disagreed among themselves, but a clear majority in parliament were quite clear that bishops, deans and cathedrals, representative as they saw it of an unbiblical theology, had to go. From the beginning of the Civil War in 1642 those political voices became stronger and the outcome of the fighting made the dissolution of the church inevitable.

Parliament, meeting nominally in the king's name, often forced his hand and actually impeached Bishop Piers as a 'desperately prophane, impious, turbulent Pilate [?Prelate]', the word turbulent perhaps a deliberate echo of Henry II's remark that brought Becket to martyrdom. Impeachment meant a spell in the Tower. A second spell followed in 1642 with ten other bishops. Church government, as represented nationally by Convocation, came to an end in 1642, the last year for many when the bishops' and archdeacons' courts in Somerset were active. Yet Bishop Piers himself obstinately continued to appoint men to vacant parishes until 1645, that is almost a year after Laud was executed, and in the same year he ordained at least three men, the last in December 1645 well over two years after his office had been abolished. He and they were taking serious risks.

By 1645 Piers was 65 years old and a marked man. He wisely retired to Sunbury near the Thames outside London, eventually leaving his palace and estates in the destructive hands of the former Anglican turned Presbyterian preacher Cornelius Burges. Committees established by Parliament turned Dean Raleigh, the canons and the vicars choral out of the cathedral, which Burges took over as a preaching house. Raleigh himself, another target of the country's leaders

Opposite page:
Not dead but sleeping.   Phil Day,
2004 (© Templar Trust)

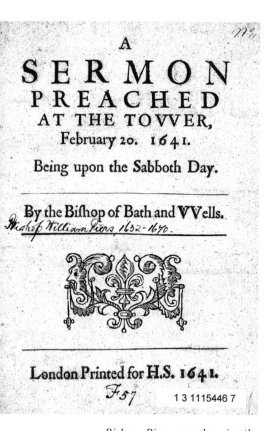

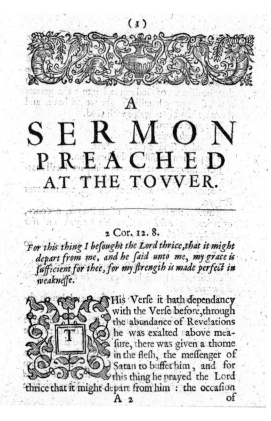

Bishop Piers preaches in the Tower, 1641. Somerset Archaeological Society

because he held with his deanery at least three other parishes and was a faithful supporter of the king, suffered vicious attacks on his person and property and in the late summer of 1646 in a scuffle with his ex-shoe-maker gaoler that might have been expected of a nephew of the great Sir Walter, was wounded and died six weeks later.

All the other cathedral prebendaries, including all three archdeacons, were also turned out of their jobs and their homes, together with ten vicars choral, for traditional cathedral services were suspended. Among the prebendaries was the bishop's son, also William Piers, archdeacon of Taunton and another marked man, as much for his political views against members of parliament as for his collection of parish livings - Buckland St Mary and Kingsbury Episcopi in addition to his rich prebend of Milverton. In exile he survived by farming, selling his cheese in the markets at Taunton and Ilminster before being sent to gaol at Ilchester, where he hung his gloves from his prison bars to encourage the charity of passers by.

Without archdeacons and senior clergy the administration of the diocese effectively collapsed: clergy and laity were no longer subject to any traditional discipline and the local administration of wills came to an end. Almost a quarter of the parishes in the diocese lost their priest, some turned out for political or theological views, others for having more than one living. Josias Alsop, rector of Norton Fitzwarren, was simply 'worried out of his living' by the presence of the garrison at Taunton. Henry Ancketyll was both a canon of Wells and rector of Mells, but his royalist views were probably his downfall, so strong that he was for a time governor of Corfe castle for the king. He died of wounds in Taunton castle. Baldwin Ackland, instituted to North Cadbury by Bishop Piers in 1643, was turned out by decision of the House of Lords two years later.

For the rest there was a long wait while a national committee tried to decide on an acceptable form of liturgy. A scheme for church government was eventually proposed along Presbyterian lines, and in sympathetic Somerset groups of parishes and their ministers (the title priest was forbidden) formed a *classis*, an assembly to establish and impose discipline and an opportunity to share the Word by preaching. Taunton was at the centre of one such group that embraced seventeen ministers from Dunster to Bridgwater and other parishes in between. Yet whatever Parliament and the Presbyterians thought, there was plenty of scope for quiet rebellion in remote country parishes where churchwardens were no longer under oath to report misdemeanours to archdeacons. Cananuel Bernard, turned out of Huish Episcopi by 1650, was left to care for Pitney and quietly, without any disturbance, conducted at least 85 weddings according to the Prayer Book for couples throughout the district. After their rector was removed from Hinton St George, also about 1650, the wardens serving under a succession of Presbyterian ministers, did the things wardens had done for generations and simply changed their titles to 'ruling elders of Hinton Church'.

Compliant or quietly rebellious, parishes were clearly affected by the Civil War and parish clerks often declared their difficulties. Entries in the parish register of Curry Rivel had been 'neglected during the time of the wars namely 1642-1650', so the clerk confessed in a typical, though not entirely satisfactory, excuse for laxity. There was a better one offered at St Mary's, Taunton, in June 1643 when it was noted by the minister or the clerk that during the siege of the town many were buried 'which were not registered'. Two years later the reason for omissions was that 'since the wars [burials] have not been set down as formerly they have been by reason there hath been no bell rung nor warening given'. The loyalist rector of Berkley seems to have taken the register with him when he was turned out in 1645 and replaced by 'alien ministers from the neighbourhood'. Some sort of order was generally restored when births, marriages and deaths were regularly recorded by each parish's Public Register, the weddings having first taken place before a Justice of the Peace.

By the mid 1650s, therefore, the church of Bishop Piers, the church of the Elizabethan settlement, had been virtually dismantled along with the monarchy. 'No bishop no king', the war-cry of the early Stuart kings, had come to pass. And yet there was a brave body of men, among them a few bold if not foolhardy bishops, who continued like the underground church of the Catholic recusants in Elizabeth's reign.

When the reinstated Bishop Piers conducted a visitation in 1670 he discovered in the diocese such men as Robert Collier at Burnham on Sea who had been made priest by Robert Skinner, bishop of Oxford, in 1648, and William Huish at Hornblotton, made deacon and priest in 1652 by Thomas Fulwar, bishop of the Irish see of Ardfert and Aghadoe. There were in Somerset in 1670 at least fourteen such men, who had been prepared to face the full rigour of the law to serve the church they held so dear. They, as well as their bishop, must have been both surprised and enormously satisfied when Charles II was restored in 1660 and the old diocesan structure was rebuilt.

The Light Shines in the Darkness

John 1.5

There must have been much satisfaction for William Piers when Charles II was restored to power and the church he had for so long struggled to preserve for the king's father was brought back by parliamentary decree. After the 'ejections' of ministers unable to accept the whole of the Book of Common Prayer, it was no longer a church for the whole nation, for they and others turned out from neighbouring dioceses led congregations calling themselves variously Congregational, Presbyterian or Baptist. Laws passed by an aggressive Anglican parliament attempted to limit their activities and over the next quarter century, between occasional outbursts of toleration, magistrates often proceeded against those nonconformists, together with Quakers, with considerable severity. Church courts, too, took what action they could and it was part of the duties of churchwardens to report those who did not attend the services of the church. Thus in 1668 widow Eleanor Matthews of Combe St Nicholas, was accused of holding meetings in her house on Sundays (clearly rivalling the service in the parish church) and of employing former ministers ('silenced preachers', they were rather mistakenly called), one of whom was probably John Baker, removed from Curry Mallet four years earlier. John

Anglicans restored: Low Ham chapel, built by George Stawell in 1668-9. The screen bears the text: My sonne feare God and the Kinge and meddle not with them that are given to change. Robert Dunning

Opposite page: *The light shines in the darkness.* Phil Day, 2004 (© Templar Trust)

103

Dyer and John Keetch, presumably for religious reasons, had not brought their children to church for baptism and they and two others had refused to pay the regular tax to maintain the parish church. At the same court in 1676 the wardens reported that 29 adults regularly failed to attend church, that three members of the Garland family were Quakers, that Alice Walter was said to be a Roman Catholic and that two women kept private schools with no approved religious teaching. In the following year 'public dissenters and fanatics' were reported again and in the next year Agnes Standerwick was holding meetings (called conventicles) in her home in the village.

Anti-Roman Catholic feelings also ran high at times, and in 1685 in part provoked the rebellion of the duke of Monmouth and in 1688 the imprisonment of seven bishops in the Tower, one of them Thomas Ken. The Revolution of 1689, when the catholic James II was replaced by the protestant William III and Mary II, a wide measure of toleration was agreed, but Ken found himself unable to take an oath of loyalty to the new monarchs while his previous king still lived. He and a few Somerset clergy joined the ranks of the dispossessed 'non-jurors', while others with Jacobite sympathies, still favouring the exiled James II, remained in post. Many were the laymen, too, who taking advantage of the law attended their parish church but also worshipped in their nonconformist meeting houses, among them one or two leading members of Bridgwater's ruling corporation.

The rebellions of 1715 and 1745 kept the possibility of a Roman Catholic comeback alive in the hearts of a few but attention was drawn for the most part to wars against the French and Spanish and, at the end of the century, the great struggle against Napoleon. The Church of England, ignoring rather than actively opposing the spreading nonconformist churches, was yet by no means as lifeless as is often suggested, continuing with its ancient structures of government but profoundly affected by a rebirth of spiritual activity that the diehards called 'enthusiasm'. It was the success of the Wesleys and their like that eventually brought awareness that the church was no longer connected with many of its people and laid the foundation for revival in the nineteenth century.

BISHOPS BACK ON THEIR THRONES

William Piers came back to power at the age of 80. Resignation on a pension was not an option, though since 1655 he had been living in retirement just outside Oxford. He spent £5,000 on repairs to his palace at Wells to put right the damage done by Burges and gave the cathedral £400 towards its repairs, but whether he came to the diocese at all and if so how long he stayed is not known. He conducted regular ordinations from 1662 to 1669 but they may have taken place at his home at Walthamstow in Essex where he lived with his much younger second wife. He died there in 1670, at 90 the oldest bishop in Christendom.

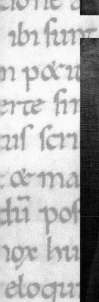

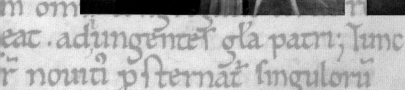

Clockwise from top left:

William Piers (bishop 1632-70), artist unknown but datable to 1660-70, hardly an accurate representation of a man in his eight- ies. Bishop's Palace, Wells

Peter Mews (bishop 1673-84) as bishop of Winchester, perhaps after Michael Dahl, 1706. Bishop's Palace, Wells

Richard Kidder (bishop 1691-1703), artist unknown after an original by Mary Beale at Emmanuel college, Cambridge. Bishop's Palace, Wells

Thomas Ken (bishop 1685-90) by F Scheffer, 1711. Bishop's Palace, Wells

After the very short rule of Robert Creighton (1670-72), formerly dean of Wells, Peter Mews arrived, a Dorset man whose previous career as royalist soldier, spy, political plotter and diplomat clearly fitted him for his later roles as archdeacon, dean and bishop. He proudly bore a patch proclaiming a noble wound, one of several received in the Civil War when he served as a captain in the king's forces. One of his enemies, himself a bishop, declared he owed his successful clerical career to 'obsequiousness and fury', but while he was certainly often furious - he was vehement against nonconformists, whose ringleaders in Somerset, he promised, 'shall have no quarter from me' - his brave and faithful service to the crown in exile clearly deserved reward. And Mews could certainly be diplomatic, declaring during a dispute with the cathedral that he wrote a letter personally because religion and charity commanded his passion and he signed himself 'Your affectionate, though at present affronted Brother'.

Mews was translated to Winchester in 1684 and was followed by the king's personal, if somewhat quixotic, choice of Thomas Ken ('the little black fellow who refused Nelly a lodging'), another loyal Tory but always a clergyman. Ken was a man of prayer and principal, and is commemorated for those qualities in the church's calendar of saints. His humble generosity to the poor, his care for rebel prisoners following the Monmouth rebellion, and above all his stand against the means by which William and Mary came to power, have brought him a prominence that he would have shunned. Others, notably Bishop Arthur Lake, had been equally humble and generous to the poor, and even the warlike Peter Mews had urged restraint on the judges dealing with Monmouth's supporters. Ken, who with Archbishop Sancroft and five other bishops had been imprisoned in the Tower for resisting James II's policies, found himself in conscience unable to take the oath of loyalty to William and Mary and, in the words of his registrar, 'was according to an Act of Parliament ... deprived'. Ken declared he would leave his diocese 'with greater cheerfulness, then [sic] I at first accepted it'.

Potentially, of course, Ken could have been at the head of an underground continuing church, and there were those who thought that the exiled James II had made him archbishop of Canterbury. Instead, he lived quietly, sometimes staying at Yeovilton Rectory with Archdeacon Edwin Sandys, keeping in touch with his many friends; he refused to return to his old diocese when Bishop Kidder died in 1703, saw out his days at Longleat and was buried in the churchyard of Frome in 1711.

Richard Kidder also did not want to be a bishop. He knew he would meet with 'great trouble and envy' and clearly did not relish his responsibilities, though he took them very seriously. His enemies - and in his rather sad autobiography he repeatedly referred to them – thought him too liberal (latitudinarian was the current word) and too sympathetic to former nonconformists; and for high church Tories he was a government stooge. Yet he was clearly both a scholar and a

Tomb of Bishop Ken in the churchyard of St John's, Frome, designed by Benjamin Ferrey 1844. Robert Dunning

Clockwise from top left:

George Hooper (bishop of Bath and Wells 1704-27), artist unknown; a reduced version of the 1723 original by Thomas Hill, Christchurch, Oxford. Bishop's Palace, Wells

John Wynne (bishop of Bath and Wells 1727-43), artist unknown, reduced version about 1730 of portrait at Jesus college, Oxford. Bishop's Palace, Wells

Edward Willes (bishop of Bath and Wells 1743-73) by Thomas Hudson about 1747. Bishop's Palace, Wells

Charles Moss (bishop of Bath and Wells 1774-1802), by John Hoppner, about 1800. Bishop's Palace, Wells

Richard Beadon (bishop of Bath and Wells 1802-24), artist unknown after original by Francis Lemuel Abbott at Jesus college, Cambridge, 1789-1802. Bishop's Palace, Wells

conscientious bishop, not willing, as many were, to appoint men to parishes because they asked or had influence. His death during the great storm of 1703 was a shock even to those who disliked him.

George Hooper had a fine start to a glittering career, successively chaplain to Bishop Morley at Winchester and to Archbishop Sheldon, followed by service with Princess (later Queen) Mary in Holland. He came to Wells in 1704 at the age of 63 after a very short spell as absentee bishop of St Asaph, to which post he had been appointed through the influential Tory politician Robert Harley. He was a formidable scholar and clerical politician whose high church views gradually changed as moderates came to power. Ken expressed personal approval of him (they had been the bishop's chaplains together at Winchester), considering he could do 'excellent service to this sinking church'. In fact it was Ken who persuaded him to accept Wells and Hooper in return managed to negotiate a pension for Ken. Hooper was later offered both the archbishopric of York and the bishopric of London but declined both. He died in 1727 at the age of 87 at Berkley House, near Frome, the home of his daughter.

Birth and patronage together were a formidable combination for promotion in the eighteenth century. John Wynne, who succeeded Hooper, was a Welshman with a legendary pedigree and was a considerable scholar - Lady Margaret professor of divinity and then principal of Jesus college, both in Cambridge. He, too, tried out his skills on the diocese of St Asaph, the first bishop to be appointed by George I, and came to Wells at the age of 60, but his heart remained in Wales and he died at his home at Soughton, in Flintshire, in 1743.

Edward Willes was almost certainly a political appointee but an active dean of Lincoln and for a year or so bishop of St David's. His elder brother just happened to be a senior judge, but he had also himself been of assistance to the government of the day in the curious office of 'Decypherer to the King', evidently involving Jacobite correspondence. Willes was bishop in Somerset for nearly 30 years and died at his fashionable London home in 1773 at the age of 79. He was buried in the cloister of Westminster Abbey where he had been a prebendary before his consecration as bishop.

Charles Moss was a Norfolk man who also came via two fashionable London parishes and the see of St David's. His burial at Grosvenor Chapel, South Audley Street, London, at the age of 90 in 1802 suggests that, as for Bishop Willes, Wells was not his favourite home. Richard Beadon, by contrast, was almost a Somerset man, his father having moved to Devon from Brushford. His appointment as tutor to William, duke of Gloucester, brother of George III, was a guarantee of promotion but he served for some years as a tutor at St John's college, Cambridge, and then as head of Jesus college there. In 1789 he was made bishop of Gloucester and in 1802 he came to Wells, where he remained until his death in 1824 at the age of 87.

THE WORK OF THE BISHOP

The regular duties of a post-Restoration bishop were essentially the same as they had ever been. The winter months were largely to be spent in London to attend parliament, the summer in Somerset with a regular round of confirmations and visitations in the central churches of each deanery, preaching then and on other special occasions, visiting what remained of the estates that provided his income, and presumably dining with social equals. In between there were clergy to interview, disputes to be pursued, sinners to be corrected, sometimes with, but often without, the cooperation of his legal and secretarial staff, the archdeacons and the cathedral prebendaries. In fact a bishop, as Kidder found, could so easily be isolated, unable to offer significant leadership or pursue any kind of policy in the face of men appointed to positions of power and financial attraction by his predecessors and for life. No wonder Willes, Moss and Beadon all appointed their sons to offices of significance; it was some sort of guarantee of an easier existence.

The upheavals of the 1640s and 1650s and the losses of clergy in 1660 and 1662 led to a shortage of acceptable men and the danger of falling standards. Bishop Mews surprised some of his critics when he deplored the ignorance he found among the Somerset clergy and Bishop Kidder was probably not the only one to expose a man producing forged papers to gain ordination. At every visitation bishops required details of the education of the clergy, their ordination, posts held and the justification (legal rather than pastoral) for holding more than one living. The visitations, involving both much travelling around the diocese and much exhausting ceremony, were clearly too much for ageing bishops, who often delegated the duty to deputies known as surrogates or commissaries, though Bishop Moss continued to visit in person until the age of 86, remarkably covering one third of the

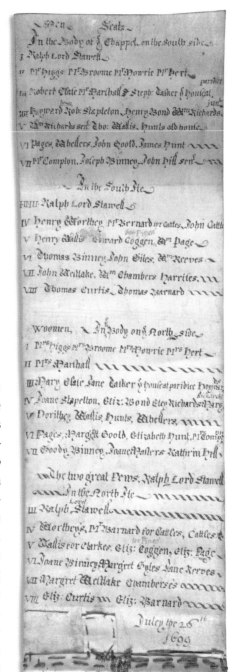

Copies of baptisms, marriages and burials taken from parish registers were to be sent to the bishop each year: 'bishop's transcripts' from Wilton for the year 1663. The churchwardens noted 'Noe mynister in our parish'. Somerset Record Office D/D/Rr 467.

Left: *Ownership of pews at Low Ham, 1699. Women were assigned seats in the north aisle. Somerset Record Office DD/MKG 16*

Seating arrangements at Catcott in the later seventeenth century: men on the south side, women on the north. Robert Dunning

diocese every year. A century earlier Bishop Mews was no doubt gratified when the bells of West Buckland rang out to greet him when he went to visit his tenants in the parish in 1680.

Ordinations and appointments to parishes, recorded in due legal form by the bishop's registrar, are by the seventeenth century the only regular record of a bishop's activities. At his first ordination after his restoration, on 22 December 1662, Bishop Piers ordained 7 priests and made 16 men deacons. Bishop Mews priested 12 men and made 18 deacons in his first two ordinations in his cathedral and over the next four months held four more, two at St Sepulchre's in London while he was there on parliamentary business; and two in the chapel of St John's college in Oxford, where he was still president and vice-chancellor of the university. Otherwise, so far as the registrar recorded the fact, he ordained sometimes in the chapel of the Holy Trinity in the palace at Wells, sometimes in the cathedral. Bishop Ken ordained a total of 23 priests in eight services, also either in the palace chapel or the cathedral. Bishop Kidder recorded in his autobiography how seriously he took the rite of ordination, as surely Bishop Ken did before him. He rejected unsuitable candidates with the greatest possible tact and at Trinity 1693 he recalled how both he and his chaplain subjected one man to the most careful examination. Possession of a university degree did not, of course, qualify a man to be a pastor, and Kidder had hopes, unfulfilled, to involve the cathedral chapter as some kind of training college. Bishop Hooper in just over twenty years ordained 214 priests and his daughter recorded that very few were without university training and the total figure almost certainly included men rejected at least once who were sometimes given money to support further study.

There are no such records of confirmations, just as in the Middle Ages and later, but it is impossible to believe that Ken, the pastor who wrote hymns for pupils at Winchester college, did not take the rite seriously. It was, after all, the best possible way of meeting and talking to the ordinary people of the diocese. Bishop Kidder held regular confirmations in the market towns, probably linked with visitations. At Bridgwater in 1693, after previous instruction and examination by local clergy, he was faced with 'a vast appearance' of candidates. He found the process 'painful and wearisome' but was certain he had done no better day's work in his life. His enemies remembered the day because he went to dinner with the town's Presbyterian mayor. Three of his successors, Wynne, Willes and Moss, in face of their ill health or age persuaded neighbouring bishops to conducted the mammoth proceedings that were common in the eighteenth century and in October 1822 the bishop of Gloucester took the place of the sick Richard Beadon at a ceremony in Bath Abbey when 1233 people were confirmed. Six years later the much more energetic Bishop Law confirmed 'multitudes' from the Frome area that took 'upwards of two hours'.

Bishop Kidder in 1693 at Bridgwater was spared the duty of a sermon at the confirmation for the vicar of Woolavington preached and subsequently published his work. Bishop Ken before him was remembered for his 'very edifying way of preaching, but ... more apt to move the passions than instruct the reason, and though his manner of doing it was very taking, yet there always appeared more beauty than solidity to his sermons'. That was one point of view. He asked that two sermons he preached in Bruton on 6 November 1687 'all persons them remember'. His teaching had already in 1684 been made clear in his Exposition on the Church-Catechism, in a much simpler book for the use of the poor, and in prayers for those going to Bath to take the waters. One or two of Kidder's sermons were printed on such subjects as fasting and wilful sins; a more significant one was a 'discourse' he had composed 'in a plain and easy style, suited to the meanest capacity' and 'for the poorer inhabitants' of his diocese. It was, so the bishop planned, to be distributed in great numbers, but publication was delayed by his sudden death. Bishop Moss only published one sermon after he came to Wells, preached before the Society for the Propagation of the Gospel in 1776 and Bishop Beadon two.

THE BISHOP'S STAFF

Post-Reformation bishops of Bath and Wells, while deprived of some of their estates, still had a substantial income, amounting in Bishop Hooper's time to some £885. Apart from domestic staff each would have a registrar to ensure that the appointments of clergy were made and recorded correctly and who, with deputies, acted as adviser to the courts of the diocese. And he would also have a chancellor, usually a clerical lawyer and his principal secretary, who might also be the presiding judge of the bishop's court, known as the vicar-general and official principal. His was usually an appointment for life and he would thus be 'inherited' by a succeeding bishop.

Bishop Ken's vicar general, John Bayley, and his registrar, Guy Clinton, had both been in office for at least ten years by 1688. Bishop Kidder's staff formed an unhappy group, in 1694 falling out about the fees each claimed from church business and clearly not agreeing with their employer.

A much more deeply damaging dispute arose in the 1730s, continued until 1740 and rumbled on until the death of the principal protagonist in 1753. It began when Chancellor Thomas Eyre, clergyman, lawyer and vicar-general, and presumably appointed chancellor by Bishop Wynne, took exception to the official activities of Archdeacon Atwood of Taunton, challenging his age-old right to hold visitations and to prove wills. He then subverted the bishop's own authority by a series of actions and sentences in the bishop's own court with the result that all three archdeacons were excommunicated, the cathedral virtually closed, and the administrative work of the whole diocese brought to a halt. Poor Bishop Wynne had himself to seek legal advice as to how to act against his own legal self for, said a lawyer he consulted, 'he had not power enough left to protect his friends'.

Perhaps to ensure there was no repetition of such a crisis, but also to provide some financial support for his family, Bishop Willes appointed his eldest son Edward, a lawyer and royal decypherer, to succeed the turbulent Thomas Eyre. Chancellor Willes served until 1788, well into

Was a faculty issued or even applied for? Mid-seventeenth-century alabaster font, Elworthy.
Robert Dunning

the time of Bishop Moss, though his place in the courts in the 1760s had usually been taken by a surrogate or deputy, Francis Potter, who happened also to be archdeacon of Wells. After Willes as chancellor came Charles Moss, a recent graduate and appointed for life by his father. Dr Moss continued to be nominal chancellor and vicar-general while he from 1807 was himself bishop of Oxford. Bishop Beadon appointed his only son and namesake Richard, a layman, to succeed in 1812, and he remained in office until 1827.

A rather similar attitude was taken by bishops when they appointed archdeacons. Bishop Piers' son and namesake became archdeacon of Bath in 1638 and of Taunton in 1643, and his support seems to have been available to succeeding bishops until his death in 1682. Bishop Mews appointed Edwin Sandys to be archdeacon of Wells in 1683 and he proved a great friend to Bishop Ken but, as a Tory and continuing supporter of the exiled James II, he absolutely refused to cooperate with Bishop Kidder. Chancellor Eyre saw all three archdeacons as his, but not necessarily the bishop's, opponents in the 1730s, and from then onwards Willeses, Mosses and Beadons (and Willes sons-in-law Seaman and Aubery) held most of the lucrative and prestigious offices in the cathedral well into the nineteenth century, three of them archdeacons of Wells between 1749 and 1815 and two of them archdeacons of Taunton. Evidently a family business.

The courts of bishop and archdeacon continued as they had done for centuries, sitting every week during the Law Terms usually in the little room under the cathedral's north-west tower, though occasionally at the convenience of the presiding judge in his own house. Successive chancellors, holding the fine title of vicar-general and official principal or some variation, heard, in person or by deputy, the kind of cases that had been heard in the Middle Ages - failing to pay tithe, slanderous remarks made in public, clerical misbehaviour, arrangements for or disputes about marriage, and the business of wills and their administration. Just occasionally the court gave permission (by faculty) for changes in church buildings and furniture, such as when in 1726 a gallery was permitted in Bridgwater church, or in 1795 when a small chantry chapel and porch on the south side of Queen Charlton church were allowed to be demolished and a new porch built. The court's proceedings were recorded in Latin until 1730.

Bishop Kidder sat personally in his court beside his chancellor when he demanded to know why Daniel Ballow, vicar of Chard and parish priest of Crewkerne, refused his order to give up one or the other. At the height of Chancellor Eyre's extraordinary dispute with the archdeacons the bishop managed to get hold of the court records and had business transferred to the palace, where he heard the case the churchwardens of Midsomer Norton brought against a recalcitrant parishioner. If all this sounds now quite bizarre, it must be clear that even in such a formal way the bishop's court was part of the way the church continued to make a contribution to the stability of society at a time when alternative religious or secular attractions were all too apparent.

THE LIGHT SHINES IN THE DARKNESS

The archdeacon of Wells kept his regular court in the cathedral's south transept, 'near the font', and on his visitations within each deanery often used its principal church as a place of meeting. Somerton had an archdeacon's pew for the purpose. Archdeacon Archer presided with his registrar before the clergy, wardens and sidemen of Frome deanery in Frome parish church on 9 October 1738. The registrar called the names of those summoned, administered the oath of office to the new holders and also took the oath of the parish's new clerk. Two days later at Bruton the procedure was repeated and the registrar reminded himself in his book that he had received the full fee for issuing the summons. At Yeovil six days later one of the sidemen of Poyntington (then still in the diocese) failed to appear and was reprimanded. In the following Spring, back at Bruton, Mr Baldwin Malet preached the visitation sermon, John Wynne of East Pennard was reported to be absent in Chard and only a very small fee had been paid. The registrar also noted that there was an outbreak of 'very bad distemper' in Yeovil, so Merston deanery was avoided. A second visit to Cary deanery in the Autumn, planned for Ansford, was cancelled because of the archdeacon's death.

A visitation of the archdeaconry of Taunton in 1753 after the death of George Atwood began under his deputy at Crewkerne on 29 September when the rector of Swell and vicar of Fivehead (one and the same) and his wardens were reported absent and the whole session seems to have been postponed for three days. Chancellor Eyre, typically, then stepped in, almost the last act of his life. Sessions went on to Taunton and Bridgwater over the next six days. A small calculation at the end of the record noted that churchwardens had made their statutory reports in writing (called presentments) - sometimes complaints, usually 'all well'- for which they had been charged a fee of two shillings each. The registrar's deputy pocketed the respectable sum of £11 12s (£11.60p) for 116 responses. Wardens in Wells archdeaconry in the same year turning up late for the court session had to look for Archdeacon Potter either at the Angel at Axbridge or at the Ansford Inn. The wardens of Milton Clevedon and Shepton Montague had better things to do at Hindon Fair.

Deaneries, those most ancient of groups of parishes, seem to have continued their unbroken history, but exactly what rural deans were doing is rather a mystery. The deans of Merston are briefly glimpsed in a curious entry in the Milborne Port registers in 1605 but no more is heard until 1665 when Archbishop Sheldon of Canterbury sent an enquiry about clergy, lecturers, schools, medical practitioners and nonconformists. The deanery was clearly a manageable unit and a bundle of thirty answers has survived for Cary deanery, all sent to the rural dean, Richard Squire, rector of Blackford. Two other clues to rural deans bring their story to the beginning of the nineteenth century. One refers to the regular annual meeting of rural deans, probably in the late 1720s, at which they distributed charity money to poor clergy and their families; the other is a remark made by a West Somerset clergyman in 1803 that Mr Parsons, the rector of Goathurst and Wembdon, was rural dean 'and examines churches'.

Ilminster church in the mid eighteenth century. Somerset Archaeological Society

THE STATE OF THE DIOCESE

In the late 1770s, presumably on the initiative of Bishop Moss, a questionnaire was sent out to each parish. It was not, apparently, returned very promptly so the exact date of each answer is not certain. The bishop wanted to know the number of communicants, as some guide to the strength of the church in each parish, and also the activities of Roman Catholics, Presbyterians, Baptists, Quakers and Methodists. He also enquired about schools and support for the poor. What the bishop thought of the answers is not known, but it was clear that while some church congregations were thriving, so, too, were others, particularly in the growing towns and industrial areas. No

St Swithin, Walcot, Bath, designed by Thomas Jelly and John Palmer and built 1777-80. It was almost immediately extended eastwards by two bays and given tower and spire by 1790. Robert Dunning

reply from St Peter and St Paul parish (now Bath Abbey) has survived, but St Michael's in Broad Street reported there were commonly 50 or 60 communicants and at festivals from 140 to 150. At Bathwick, then hardly developed, there were 14 communicants, but at rapidly-expanding Walcot about 300. As for the other churches and chapels, there were some 'reputed papists' in St Michael's parish, many Presbyterians with their own minister and a meeting-house duly licensed (either by the bishop or the magistrates as the law required), in Bathwick none and in Walcot about ten Roman Catholic families, six Quaker families, six Presbyterian, a licensed Moravian chapel and two Methodist chapels. Both St Michael's and Walcot parishes had a school, the former the Edward VI grammar school, the latter a charity school for boys and girls supported by collections in church.

Across the diocese there were similar contrasts and some unexpected answers. Keynsham had between 40 and 50 communicants, Long Ashton 60, Berrow 50, Beckington between 80 and 100, Frome between 300 and 400. Obscure Rodden had 'seldom less than 40', Chiselborough between 20 and 30, West Chinnock between 30 and 40'. As for other towns, Somerton had 'about 100', Yeovil the same but on the great festivals more, Bridgwater 100, Crewkerne about 70, Chard about 40, the two churches in Taunton together 70, Glastonbury 'uncertain'. Surprising numbers were reported at Kingston St Mary with 100 and South Petherton with 70-90, perhaps reflecting the enthusiasm of Wesley's sympathisers in the two parishes.

At the other end of the scale, well over fifty churches had fewer than ten communicants, among them the three coastal parishes of Clevedon, Weston super Mare and Portishead, not yet risen to the status of seaside resorts; five recording as few as three communicants and Chilton Trinity not enough to attend because there were only three houses in the parish. Five among the small congregations survived into the late twentieth century and were then declared redundant for lack of sustained support.

Schools were to be found in 45 parishes, charities for the poor in 40. Cucklington had one of each because of the endowment that provided cash to send two poor boys to learn to read well in the Bible. In two places there were particular signs that clergy had recognised the pastoral problem facing the church and had risen to the challenge. A lively rector at Ashwick had founded a charity to ensure that a sermon was preached every Sunday and at Paulton another had made sure that what he called 'additional duty', that is another service, would be provided, evidently to discourage his people from attending the Baptist chapel.

In 1810 Bishop Moss presumably approved a second enquiry that asked three simple questions: how many Church of England churches and chapels were there in the parish, how many people did they hold, and how many other chapels were in use. Answers from only 55 parishes have survived including all the Bath parishes, but only the vicar of Crewkerne actually went to the crux of the matter, for he also gave the population of his parish, 2500, and he remarked that 'even

The Sunday School at Edington, built 1772. Robert Dunning

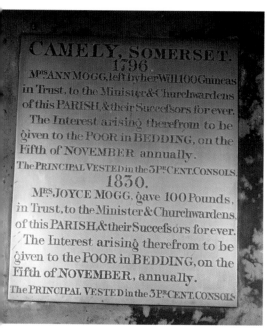

Cameley charities. Robert Dunning

in its present unfinished state' his church could hold 2000 and 'when the pews are fitted up to advantage' all parishioners. The one dissenting chapel in Crewkerne, built about 70 years earlier, would then, he presumably hoped, be out of business.

By 1810 the Church of England 'proprietary chapels' of Bath, private commercial ventures for popular preachers where members paid a subscription providing for their minister and their seats, were doing good business: the Octagon Chapel in Milsom Street had room for about 600, Argyle chapel in Bathwick for nearly 2000, and five in Walcot including Kensington chapel for a total of 3703. Wesleyans, Moravians and members of Lady Huntingdon's chapel in Walcot parish had seats for 2210. By contrast St James's in the city could hold about 800 of a total population of 4000, and a similar total in Bathwick had a church that would hold no more than 200 and was 'in a most dilapidated state'. It was rebuilt in 1817-20. The Abbey had room for about 1000 and its minister reported a meeting room newly opened in Parsonage Lane.

Elsewhere in the diocese, as in Walcot, nonconformist chapels were growing in size and number. At Shepton Mallet the parish church could hold 1500 before being widened and given galleries in 1837 but four chapels held 1790 people. The balance in Taunton St Mary was 4000 in the parish church and 3500 in four chapels. The vicar of Ilminster claimed, with apparent satisfaction, that his church held 350, his parish population was 2000, but there were no other places of worship. The vicar of South Petherton remarked that there were 'too many' other places of worship, for about half of his parishioners were dissenters.

The third survey was organised by Bishop Beadon but was ordered by the Privy Council. It took the form of a printed letter directed to each rector or vicar, and to it was attached a series of questions designed to discover which of them was resident, what services were held, and the state of the house he lived or should have lived in. If he was an absentee, what was the reason and who looked after his people in his absence? The year was 1815, by which date other bishops had already realised that the work of the church was clearly being hampered because so many parishes had no regular clergyman, that two services each Sunday assumed by the Prayer Book were frequently not held, and that many of the clergymen who led those services were badly-paid curates who, sometimes nicknamed gallopers, spent their Sundays riding from one place to another trying both to oblige their absentee employers and to make even a passable living.

To be absent was not unlawful; the bishop's permission was sufficient just as it had been in the Middle Ages, and was given provided that the law permitted it, the request seemed reasonable and a substitute adequate. Unlike the Middle Ages, the supply of clergy was inadequate, hence gallopers. But when, as in 1815 in this diocese, absentees were reported as holding nearly half the parishes and a significant number had no curate, then the mission of the church, if it could be said to have a conscious mission in such circumstances, was not likely to be successful.

Duty and decency were watchwords of clerical behaviour. It was the squire's duty to appoint a proper clergyman to serve his family living and the duty of every patron to do the same. The squire's younger son was often eminently suitable. It was the parson's duty (in person or employing a curate) to serve that parish, to conduct the lawful services - morning and evening (actually afternoon) prayer and quarterly communions - to baptise, marry and bury all those who had not positively turned their backs on the church. It was his duty, too, to be involved with the churchwardens in the government of the parish, for they were responsible for the fabric and furniture of the church, for supporting the poor and the sick, for administering charities, occasionally running a school, employing a clerk and a sexton, paying the bell-ringers for celebrating royal occasions, victories on land and sea and of course commemorating that dreadful plot on 5 November and the

Nettlecombe church and manor house in close partnership: a Ralegh probably built the church, Trevelyans extended it, and Trevelyans and their relations were rectors continuously between 1724 and 1851. Robert Dunning

day (29 May) when King Charles came into his own again.

The wardens of every parish were required regularly to say that all in their church was decent - the parson's surplice, the Prayer Book and Bible, the 'carpet' that covered the communion table except when the 'fair linen cloth' was spread over it for communion, and (in one or two places such as Wiveliscombe) a linen sheet to clothe someone doing public penance imposed in the bishop's court. There was to be decent seating, too, in pews of suitable size and quality for which the better-off paid rent, and open benches (often women on one side of the church, men on the other) for the unmarried and the poor. James Hine obtained licence from the bishop's court in 1760 to take over a substantial part of the south aisle of Bishop's Hull church over which to build a private pew for his family and their successors as occupiers of Barr House, and under it to make a vault in which to bury them.

The services were hardly stimulating, for the parson read the required words and the clerk made the responses. The children of squire and parson may have been examined on the subject of the sermon when they reached home but the rest of the parishioners did not expect to understand a word. In a sharp dispute in Bridgwater in the 1690s involving a man who attended the parish church as the law required but was also a leading Presbyterian, a witness in court said he carefully made his responses to the services 'loud enough to be heard of anyone near him (if not asleep)' while his accuser 'doth usually sleep or lie in a sleeping posture … and therefore 'tis no wonder if he does not hear the responses'.

The wardens of Wiveliscombe were not alone when in 1712 they paid for a bell 'to wake the people in church' and a man to ring it; and the sexton of Henstridge was required 'to walk the church with his whip and bell in the time of divine service to observe that people did not sleep'. The vicar and wardens of Dulverton, however, went to some expense to improve worship by going to the bishop's court in 1762 and getting approval for the vicar and the squire to swap a small part of the chancel for a similar piece of the nave so that the reading desk might no longer be at 'too great a distance from the congregation'.

'In Quires and Places where they sing' the Prayer Book permitted a place at morning and evening prayer for an anthem and the creed could be said or sung; but by the 1660s few parish churches had organs and the nearest things to hymns were metrical psalms. Somerton's organ, first mentioned in the late 1630s, was dismantled in the 1650s but was still remembered in 1689 when a seat in the chancel was described as 'under the place where the organs stood'. At St Cuthbert's in Wells the singing gallery was taken down early in 1727 and replaced with an organ loft. Yet singing, presumably unaccompanied, continued in some fashion, though at Abbas Combe the singers left the church to join the dissenters and the parish vestry (the equivalent of the P.C.C.) decided in 1720 to employ someone from Henstridge to teach ten people to take their places.

A row of 'hatpins' for the use of gentlemen attending Cameley. The painting of St Christopher was presumably covered by plaster when they were installed.
Robert Dunning

Thirty years later they offered a man from Mere a contract to teach singing to anyone willing to learn for they believed that a musical service would be 'a means to draw young people to church'. The singing gallery permitted at Huish Champflower in 1795 was one of many to appear in the last thirty years of the eighteenth century.

All that sounds very much like 'enthusiasm', that attitude which many felt to be beyond duty and exceeding decency. Enthusiasm was the result of introducing the notion of personal commitment to duty and emotion to decency. Thomas Coke, curate of South Petherton, who met John Wesley at Kingston St Mary vicarage in 1776, upset his vicar by his enthusiasm in inviting all and sundry to receive frequent communion. The vicar at first banned him from preaching

Sutton Montis choir, 1827; drawing by H J S 1898. Somerset Archaeological Society

in church and then dismissed him from his post after a 'nocturnal brawl' followed one of his sermons in a private house in the village. Coke later became a Methodist bishop in America but throughout his life advocated the union of his church with the Church of England.

John Wesley himself frequently visited Somerset from 1739 and found the growing communities in the Mendip mining districts particularly responsive to his message, and many lives were clearly changed. The rector of Midsomer Norton and the vicar of Kingston St Mary were among his shamefully rare supporters in the diocese, and he noted in his journal how the curate of Buckland Dinham had 'provided a mob with horns, and other things convenient, to prevent the congregation's hearing me'.

James Woodforde spent time studying the Greek New Testament in the weeks before his ordination in Oxford in 1761 and in his first months as a curate he noted, entirely without emotion, how he read prayers and preached on Sundays, conducted a funeral (10s 6d (52p) for the sermon), churched a new mother. What he preached about he never recorded though he noted a sermon he had heard at Castle Cary on the subject of public against private interest involved in the purchase of a fire engine. Services at Bath Abbey regularly involved visiting clergy who, if eminent, were encouraged to preach on behalf of local charities. One clerical visitor approved of prayers read with 'great judgement and exactness' but found the sermon of one visiting archdeacon satisfactory as to content but 'extremely ill' performed because the preacher fancied himself as an orator. Duty and decency were a matter of individual opinion.

The congregation at the Abbey raised over £63 for the local charity schools on a Sunday in 1766; St Michael's in the city produced a little less than £21, Walcot not £7, but the Presbyterians over £14. All suggest pews well filled, the Abbey itself a considerable draw for visitors. In the countryside the better-off parishioners attended to show an example to their tenants and employees and came on Sacrament Sundays when better-quality wine was on offer. The poor, on their benches at the back or in the gallery, were distinguished from their betters by the cheaper wine given on another Sunday. And the table to which they were all invited had a new aspect: a classical reredos to match the classical monuments on the walls, for the squire had been on the Grand Tour and the parson was steeped in classical literature. Here was religion enlightened but restrained and unemotional.

The early-eighteeenth-century Langton family memorial, Newton St Loe, 'worthy of Westminster Abbey' (Pevsner). Robert Dunning

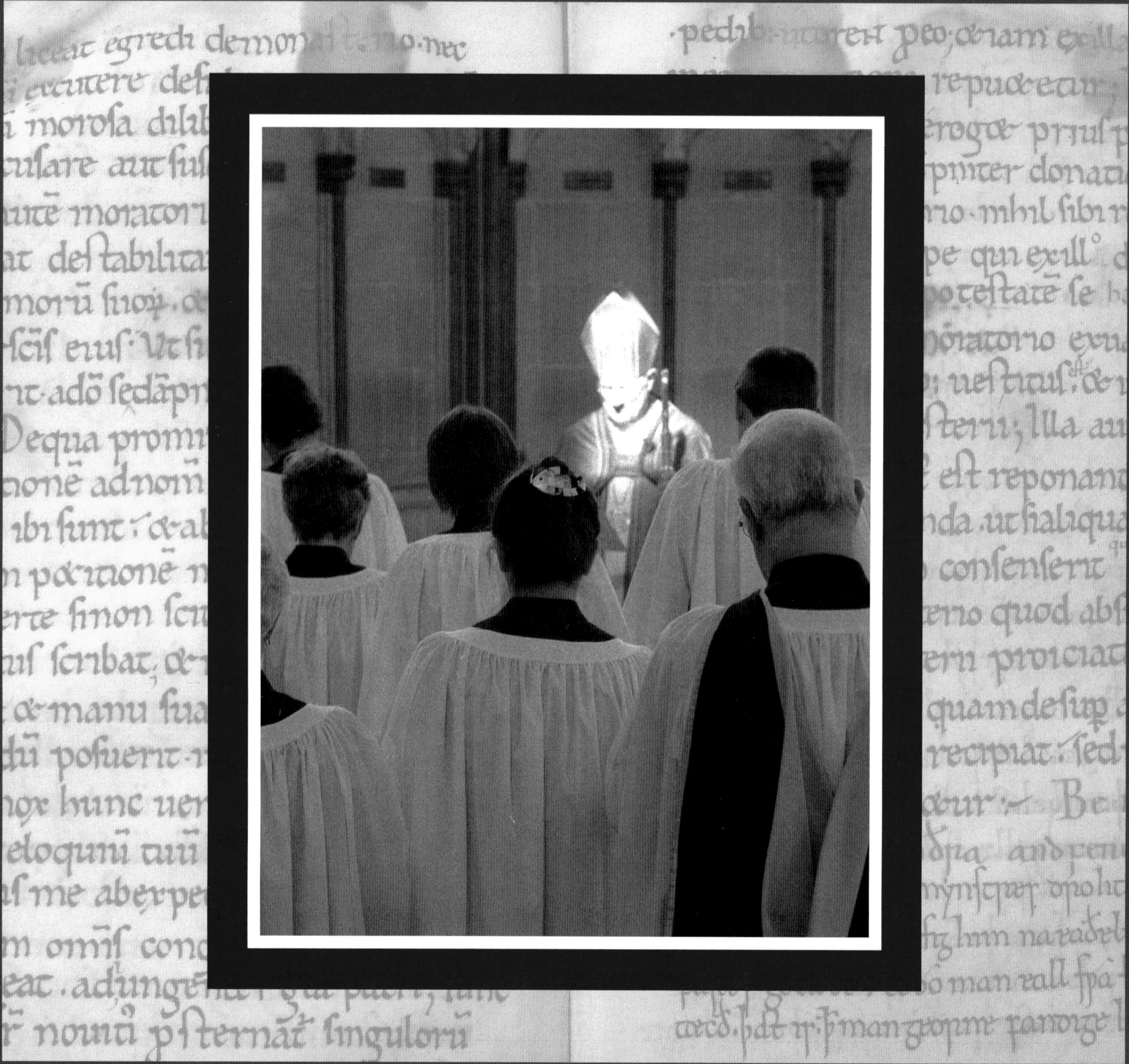

10

Fire to Give Them Light

Exodus 13.21

The revolutions in France and America and political and social discontent at home eventually brought the message to the Church of England that all might not be well with its own life. John Wesley and his preachers, eventually driven from its membership, had offered the message that God's love was not socially exclusive and many still in the church, arguing for example for the end of slavery and for toleration of other theological views, generally felt that communities, churches and individuals all needed change.

The enquiries made in the diocese in 1779, 1810 and 1815 were all undertaken against a background of a growing population that existing churches could not accommodate, a desperate need to educate the poor, rising crime and an awareness that clergy were often ill-housed, ill-paid and untrained, with the consequence that parishes were badly served and people not cared for.

Bath and Wells knew little of the problems bishops faced in urban and industrial districts, but changes soon came to be made that chimed in well with the national revival of church buildings and services. By 1840 the diocese had its own theological college at Wells to train clergy, a revived body of rural deans whose powers were later to be assumed again, as in the twelfth century, by professional and pastorally-dedicated archdeacons, and by a proliferation of diocesan bodies dedicated to education, church building and the improvement of clerical incomes. The movement may be said to have culminated in the emergence of a democratic outburst in which a (probably very select) body of laymen joined the clergy for discussions at diocesan and deanery levels. The story is, of course, complicated and made much more lively by the emergence of sharp divisions between evangelical and high church views and practices, bringing controversy and not a little shame to the Christian community. Yet at least one leader of the local church, Archdeacon Denison of Taunton, sought to bring high and low together in the face of what he saw as the greater threat of liberalism.

Opposite page:
Fire to give them light.
Phil Day 2004 (© Templar Trust)

123

The discontented cleric and author Stephen Hyde Cassan had declared that Bishop Beadon's 'advanced age, and the infirmities of nature, rendered him hardly competent for the last few years of his life'. The coming of George Henry Law from Chester in 1824, however, he thoroughly approved. Law came with twelve years of experience in the largest diocese in the land. He came with a reputation for building new churches, improving clerical incomes and performance including the end of non-residence, and with a concern that most churches were simply not large enough to house their parishioners. But he came at the age of nearly 63.

While in Chester diocese Law had reintroduced the practice that the bishop should 'visit' parishes every three years and had personally been to every one in an area stretching from the southern edge of Cheshire to the heart of the Lake District and across the Pennines well into Yorkshire. Yet in some ways Law was himself a contradiction: he had been the only bishop to support Robert Peel's attempt at factory reform, he was in favour of evening services and lectures to meet the spiritual needs of the poor in Manchester and Preston and, after some years in Somerset, he became acutely aware of the problems of the rural poor. Yet a very traditionalist Gloucestershire clergyman-squire described him in 1824 as 'very high in the esteem of the orthodox members of the church', for he had often spoken in the House of Lords against the removal of legal disadvantages of Roman Catholics and dissenters, and only voted with great reluctance for parliamentary reform in 1831-2 having been threatened by a mob in Bedminster (he fled in his carriage back to Wells and is said to have pulled up the palace drawbridge behind him, a good story but possibly not quite true) and then to have taken refuge in a house in Torquay. Law's last years were clouded by mental incapacity and he was forced in 1843 to hand over his duties to the bishop of Salisbury who, among many other duties, opened Hambridge church.

Law was followed at his death in 1845 by Richard Bagot, the second of four aristocrats to hold the see successively, for Law, the son of a bishop, was brother of the first Lord Ellenborough. Bagot was the third son of the first Baron Bagot and married a daughter of the earl of Jersey. He had combined the posts of dean of Canterbury and bishop of Oxford for 16 years before coming to Wells and his translation was Prime Minister Peel's way of ending that scandal. By then Bagot, rather less orthodox than Law because of his Tractarian leanings, was like Law over 60 and already 'sedentary'. He was later to become 'dilapidated in health' and lived at least part of the time at No, 7, Royal Crescent, Marine Parade, Brighton. Under a new and convenient Act of Parliament he was able to hand over his duties first in 1852 to George Trevor Spencer, formerly bishop of Madras (who resigned in 1853 after a dispute with Archdeacon Denison), and in 1854, two months before his death, to William Piercy Austin, formerly bishop of Guiana.

Bagot was succeeded as bishop of Bath and Wells by Robert John Eden who since 1847 had been bishop of Sodor and Man and who, on the death of his brother in 1849, had become the third Baron Auckland. He was probably of the high church school and something of an author, produc-

Lord Arthur Charles Hervey (bishop 1869-94); copy of original in Wells Town Hall by William Blake Richmond, 1889. Bishop's Palace, Wells

ing a pamphlet in 1843 entitled *Why not try the Weekly Offering?* inspired by the financial problems of the Society for the Promotion of Christian Knowledge, and another *Teetotalism, or which Pledge will you take?* Just before coming to Wells he published *The Churchman's Theological Dictionary.* By the late 1860s Lord Auckland, a little older than the century, was finding his duties too heavy and in 1866 appointed David Anderson, formerly bishop of Rupertsland in Canada, and James Chapman, formerly of Colombo, to help. In the next year Edmund Hobhouse, formerly of Nelson, joined him and in 1868 Bishop Chapman was made 'special commissary' with power not only to ordain clergy, confirm new members and consecrate churches and churchyards but also to make appointments to parishes.

Lord Auckland resigned in 1869, the first bishop of the diocese to do so since Bishop Barlow in 1553, and died early in 1870. He was followed by Lord Arthur Charles Hervey, fourth son of the first marquess of Bristol, formerly rector of the Hervey family living of Ickworth and Horningsheath in Suffolk and archdeacon of Sudbury. Hervey, unlike his predecessor, was a hugely energetic evangelical and spoke out 'roundly' against ritualism 'and the doctrine of the offering up of the mass' at his first visitation, exciting protests from Frome and Hambridge. The many branch railways all connected somehow with Wells enabled him to reach parts of the diocese that other bishops had not reached since the Middle Ages. He remained until his death in 1894.

CHANCELLORS, ARCHDEACONS AND RURAL DEANS

Bishop Law spread jobs among his family in the tradition of the Middle Ages. He made his second son Henry his chancellor or principal secretary, probably on his arrival at Wells, in 1826 he made him archdeacon of Wells, in 1827 vicar-general and official and commissary principal with a house in the cathedral close. In 1839 Henry resigned as vicar-general and probably as chancellor but soon became rector of Weston super Mare. He remained as archdeacon and rector, living in Wells, until appointed dean of Gloucester in 1862. Nationally, Henry Law was a leading evangelical and author of several biblical studies. The new chancellor and vicar-general in 1839 was Henry's cousin William Towry Law, but with the bishop's increasing senility his eldest son James T Law became chancellor and with Archdeacon Brymer administered the diocese. At least in his case there was never a charge of nepotism and when he submitted his resignation as the bishop's health declined further, the rural deans as a body, with the support of the archbishop of Canterbury, induced him to change his mind. A fourth Law, the bishop's third son, was appointed treasurer in the cathedral in 1829, a post he held until his death in 1884. Thus at least one member of the Law family held office in the diocese for 60 years.

W T Law resigned as vicar-general in 1851 when he became a Roman Catholic, and was succeeded by Bishop Bagot's fourth son Charles Walter, already his chancellor; his eighth son he made prebendary of Holcombe. The two brothers had been joint registrars in their father's former diocese of Oxford and were parish priests, the one in Norfolk, the other in Oxfordshire. Chancellor Bagot was still in office for some years after his father's death, though when a faculty was issued to rebuild Dunkerton church in 1859 his surrogate Arthur DuCane presided over the 'Consistorial Episcopal Court of Wells' and Thomas Parfitt, the apparitor-general, John Bowett and William Mullins, his lawful deputies, and George Bacon 'a mandatory for this purpose specially appointed' (probably a clerk from a lawyer's office who fixed an official notice on Dunkerton church door during Sunday service) were all involved in the process.

None of Lord Auckland's sons became priests, but three of Lord Arthur Hervey's did so, only one, Sydenham, finding employment in his father's diocese, first at Henton and later at Wedmore. The appointment to Wedmore caused some local criticism.

The archdeacons whom Law inherited were rather different from their eighteenth-century predecessors. Particularly active was George Trevelyan, archdeacon of Taunton 1817-27, who lived for most of the year in his Rectory at Nettlecombe and moved to the close at Wells for only part of each winter. His examination of Trull church and churchyard produced detailed and practical instructions for improvement that included finding a new Bible and Prayer Book for the minister and kneelers for communicants, and the removal of doors of cottages opening on to the churchyard. His successor, Anthony Hamilton (1827-51), gave learned advice on the law of pew ownership. Archdeacon Moysey of Bath (1820-39), who had been chosen by the heads of Oxford colleges as Bampton Lecturer in Divinity in 1818 and was thus clearly a distinguished theologian, refused to approve the plans for a proposed new church at Cleeve in Yatton parish in 1837. He combined his duties as archdeacon with care of the busy parish of Walcot. His successor at Bath, W T P Brymer (1839-52), as a prebendary of the cathedral occupied a house in the close at Wells and played an active role during the illness of Bishop Law. The best-known and notorious archdeacon of the nineteenth century was George Anthony Denison, archdeacon of Taunton 1851-96, who was also vicar of East Brent. Only because of the conflicting claims of various courts did he escape

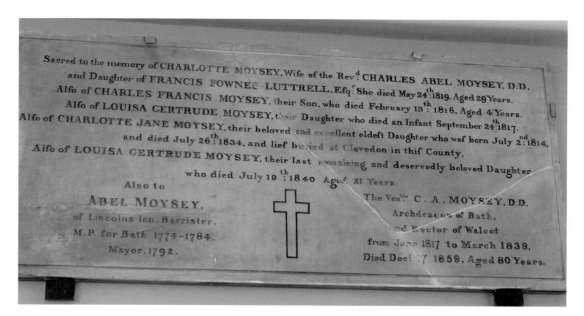

Memorial tablet to Archdeacon Moysey and his family, St Swithin, Walcot, Bath. Robert Dunning

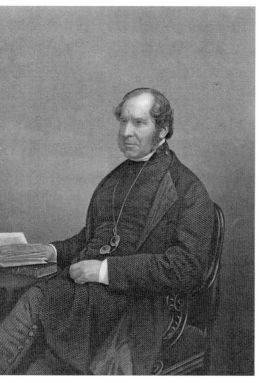

George Anthony Denison, archdeacon of Taunton 1851-96, engraved by D J Pound from a photograph by Mayall. Somerset Archaeological Society

removal from office in the 1850s because of his then unacceptable views on the eucharist. One of those pitted against him was his fellow archdeacon Henry Law of Wells and there is little doubt that Denison deliberately provoked possible martyrdom. So much for diocesan unity. Denison was certainly always to be found supporting the high church view, being present when W J E Bennett declared all seats in his church of St John at Frome to be free and no longer privately owned, and when he encouraged the eccentric Joseph Wolff to rebuild his church at Isle Brewers. He was present at the consecration of the church of St John the Evangelist, the first with entirely free seats in Taunton. And he remained in office until the age of 91.

In 1840 Bishop Law gave powers to his rural deans that they had not exercised since the Middle Ages. He asked the energetic J J Toogood, vicar of North Petherton (a member of the first Oxford boat race crew a few years before), to take over from Henry Parsons as rural dean of Bridgwater after at least 37 years and at the same time offered to make him a prebendary of the cathedral, a clear indication of the new status of the office. Toogood agreed, supposing it would not interfere with his parish duties, but almost immediately he found himself embroiled in the removal of Henry Prince from his curacy at Charlinch, the prelude to the establishment of the curious semi-religious community known as the Abode of Love at Spaxton. In a similar way the rural dean of Merston in 1846 heard evidence of the unusual behaviour of the vicar of East Coker. Thus it came about that archdeacons became concerned with practical matters such as church buildings and furnishings, drains and gutters, and the niceties of the law, and rural deans assisted the bishop in his role as Father in God.

Church courts, meanwhile, were by government decision gradually stripped of their powers: in 1843 of all questions about marriage and the administration of wills, and by 1860 remained largely to enforce proper behaviour of clergy and the legal use of and alteration to the fabric and furnishings of churches. Those powers remain in force both for the removal of disgraced clergymen and in numerous grants of faculties by the diocesan chancellor. But bishops and archdeacons continued to hold visitations, bishops every three years or so until recent years, archdeacons annually (but since 1976 not demanding the traditional fee from every parish). In 1885 the date set aside to visit the Crewkerne area was changed at the last minute when it was found that churchwardens might not attend because of the stock fair at Hinton St George.

But visitations were not, and still are not, mere formalities. 'Does your minister, properly habited, perform the services of the church as prescribed by the Book of Common Prayer, without adding, diminishing or altering?' the bishop asked in 1840. Does he do so 'audibly, distinctly, and in a devout manner, at due and seasonable hours? Does your minister instruct and examine the children in the Church Catechism at Afternoon Service?' And how many times in the year is the Holy Communion celebrated? Those questions covered the basics of the weekly service; and while positive answers were not always received in the 1840s, within forty years there had been much progress and Lord Arthur Hervey was able to say in 1885 that celebrations of communion had become 'frequent', by which he meant at least monthly and often weekly, in almost every parish, high and low. Since coming to the diocese in 1870, in fact, he had put gentle pressure on his clergy, in 1873 'earnestly requesting' that baptisms should be celebrated, as the Prayer Book required, in the time of divine service, communion at least monthly. S O Baker of Muchelney, in recording the bishop's wishes, obeyed without objection. He also recorded the names of the newly confirmed and the names - by no means the same - of the communicants, reaching a total of 25 at a celebration in 1880 and averaging just under 20 in most years to 1896.

A significant change during the nineteenth century was the emergence of the idea of 'diocese' as a force that complemented the work of individual bishops. Social and political pressure induced churchmen, both clerical and lay, to take initiatives in several important directions, particularly in work such as church extension, clerical training, and education for the poor. Much of that change was against the background of the Oxford Movement, a great revival of medieval religious experience involving new and restored buildings and liturgy and the re-emergence of the gothic style in the design of buildings. 'You must not expect much from Wells', Bishop Law wrote to the vicar of Huntspill in 1826 on receiving thanks from him for a grant for his parish school, 'We are very poor there'. Ten years later that same bishop was behind the formation of the Diocesan Church

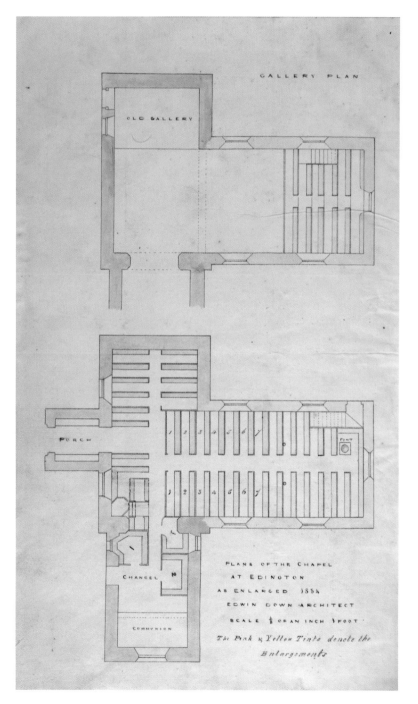

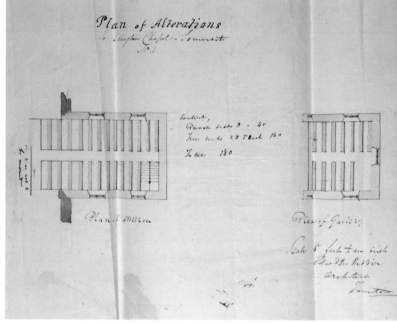

Plans of proposed extensions and galleries for Edington chapel submitted for faculty 1834 and 1878. Somerset Record Office D/P/ed 2/1/3, D/D/Cf 1878/2

Building Association in 1836 and from 1838 a Curates' Fund that began to raise money for ministry to growing working-class areas. Two years later, after a meeting at Kingweston between Henry Manning (archdeacon of Chichester and later cardinal), Archdeacon Brymer and the mildly evangelical F H Dickinson, Wells theological college began to prepare men for work as parish priests. In 1838 the Diocesan Education Society took up the work of an earlier group founded in 1812 that had given small grants for the church at East Huntspill and elsewhere and began more successfully to found new schools and to improve the standard of teaching.

Church extension in the early years of the century often involved putting in galleries like those still in place at Cameley and Evercreech or rearranging pews. J J Toogood, vicar of North Petherton, signed up for one guinea (£1.05p) to support the new Church Building Association and saw that as the opportunity to ask for help for his parish. There was some very gentlemanly dispute with the secretary of the association over the exact number of seats in the church, which they eventually agreed to be 500 in a parish with a total population of 3366. The secretary could only offer one eighth of the cost of the seats, though a greater problem were the leaks in the roof. Eventually 150 seats were added by cutting down the size of many already there and Toogood managed to get £60 from the association and the same sum from its national equivalent. The rest he raised from private subscribers.

Those details and many more are recorded in a remarkable diary Toogood kept for the first few years of his energetic ministry. The records of the Church Building Association have many

Gallery 'Erected for the Free Use of the Inhabitants. 1819' at Cameley. Robert Dunning

Galleries at Evercreech that, together with new pews, provided 239 additional seats, 149 of them free. Robert Dunning

more, from an extension to the tiny and remote Great Elm in 1837 to the work in the vast Bedminster where there was clearly not enough room in the parish church and the new church of St Paul (1829-31) and the vicar tried unsuccessfully to buy or hire the Methodist chapel. As other towns in the diocese expanded, new churches were desperately needed and were somehow built, mostly Tractarian in influence: in Bridgwater, Holy Trinity in 1839 and St John's in 1843, in Frome, Holy Trinity in 1837 and Christchurch in 1844, in Taunton, Holy Trinity in 1842 and Rowbarton (later St Andrew's) in 1844. There was similar new building in Bath, Clevedon, Wellington, Weston super Mare and Yeovil.

Churches in expanding villages like Nailsea (Holy Trinity 1843) and growing hamlets in large parishes also began to appear: at Northmoor Green in North Petherton in 1844 (for 'an almost heathen population', Mr Toogood wrote), Blackford and Theale in Wedmore, Coxley and East Horrington in Wells, Coleford in Kilmersdon, Clandown in Radstock (the last two for coal miners). And once established, such chapels were given districts of their own so that the new church communities could take decisions for themselves and become parishes in their turn: Paulton in 1841, Cleeve in Yatton in 1843.

Changes like those, and others where, for example, rich donors built East Lydford on a new and drier site in 1866 or Failand in 1887, continued at a slower pace in the second half of the nineteenth century and included rather less permanent buildings more fitted to the mission situations they served such as St Barnabas's, Welton, or Milborne Wick. They were sometimes those useful moveable structures like that serving the mining community on Brendon Hill; or the temporary home for the congregation of West Quantoxhead, displaced by building work, that migrated to Stolford and is still in use. The Word was being preached in the diocese where it had never been preached before and to people who had seldom heard it.

All that building activity required legal approval. Bishop Law had been no fan of the rather stark designs imposed on grounds of cost by those who administered government grants given for new churches. His was a more romantic nature and his treatment of the great hall of the palace at Wells and his 'cottage' at Banwell, as well as his support for the work of the architect Thomas Rickman, showed his preferences for something more than plain and utilitarian lancets - Clevedon Christchurch rather than the functional Holy Trinity, Frome. But he also knew that the bishop's legal powers had limits. In 1784 Bishop Moss had been unwilling to approve the removal of Marston Bigot church from the lawn beside the mansion to a new site some distance away, with the result that the lord of the manor and the parishioners had to petition for an Act of Parliament. Similarly Law saw a difficulty when the vicar of Huntspill asked permission to build a Sunday school on a small part of the churchyard. The bishop saw both need and opportunity, but the law did not permit him to deprive the vicar's successors of even a small amount of ancient endowment:

I most readily assent to your removing a wall of your churchyard
[Law wrote in 1826] so as to shut out a very small slip of land
you mention. My approval, I fear, however, cannot legalize the
alienation. But in so very trifling an alteration the best way is to
say nothing about it, and to let it take place sub silentio ...

But there was always a temptation to say nothing. The people of Bickenhall finally applied for a faculty to take down their church when they had already done so and had finished their new one. The faculty was duly back-dated to 1848. Charles Leir, rector of Charlton Musgrove in 1884 in succession to a long line of ancestors back to 1617, constituted himself 'chief manager and overseer' of the rebuilding of the north wall of his church. The bishop's registrar demanded proper procedure - plans, a consultation period and so on. But the only plans were in Mr Leir's head, converted to a rough sketch to keep the lawyers happy. The registrar gave way against such a forceful character but sent a clerk to serve the required papers and then issued the faculty accompanied by a bill of costs that included the clerk's expenses. Mr Leir was particularly annoyed that he had come expensively by road, having chosen a day when no train was available.

Dr E S Elwell of Chilton Polden was in close touch with the chancellor of the diocese, T E Rogers, in the spring and summer of 1888 about rebuilding, but the rector would not support the idea of any alteration to his chancel (where choir stalls were wanted) in spite of the fact that the chancel arch was in poor condition. In that case Elwell was simply too anxious to proceed and Chancellor Rogers told the registrar that Elwell was 'an over sanguine man' and would not issue a faculty until a substantial amount of the projected cost had been raised. Faith would not be sufficient for a lawyer, but the church was enlarged and partly rebuilt in the following year.

In the middle of what may be described as a mission century, a national census was taken at the end of March 1851. It was concerned with church accommodation, clergy incomes, services and attendance. The minister or church leader was responsible for answering, and the answers about attendance were deplorably vague. The curate at Wilton near Taunton said he had 'no means of giving an accurate return' and many other figures were suspiciously round. Henry Parr of St Mary's, Taunton, declared that 1205 came to morning service on 30 March 1851 of whom 205 were from the Sunday school; that 717 came in the afternoon of whom 217 were scholars, and 1450 came in the evening. There was no evening service at Holy Trinity in the town, but 700 including children were there in the morning, the same number in the afternoon. Three services at St James's had an average attendance of 584 and Rowbarton chapel had 170 in the afternoon. Thus nearly

2500 Tauntonians were at church on that Sunday morning, nearly 2000 in the afternoon, and 2200 in the evening. But Taunton was not typical, for there were as many as 12 churches of other traditions whose total congregations were over 2600 in the morning, less than 1000 in the afternoon and 2200 in the evening out of a total population of a little over 13000. Government in 1818 had decided that it was enough to provide seats for one third of the population, but in Somerset in 1851 there was seating for 40 per cent of its people, such was the progress made in the meantime.

THE CATHEDRAL

The dean and chapter of the cathedral took up church revival at a steadier pace, forced into change as much by government enquiry and Act of Parliament as by a wish to reform. Since the time of Queen Elizabeth the cathedral had been run by a body made up of eight 'residentiary' canons including a dean rather than the whole body of prebendaries, though 'residentiary' was a curious word to apply to men who lived at Wells for perhaps a month a year and still carried out their legal duties with a clear conscience. Such a man was the evangelical Henry Ryder, dean 1812-31, who from 1815 was also bishop of Gloucester and from 1824 bishop of Coventry and Lichfield. He

Henry Ryder, bishop of Gloucester and dean of Wells; engraved by T Woolnoth from a painting by H W Pickersgill. Somerset Archaeological Society

HENRY RYDER, D.D.

was, in fact, more conscientious than many contemporaries, preaching in parishes like Nether Stowey, Mark and Wedmore from which he derived some of his income, though in the opinion of some high churchmen thus letting himself down by his enthusiasm.

Ryder left the deanery in 1831, arranging to take instead a prebend at Westminster whose occupant, Edmund Goodenough, succeeded him at Wells. It was under Goodenough that the cathedral had to admit to a government enquiry into its revenues published in 1835 that the dean and six other canons residentiary took equal shares in the surplus net income of the cathedral (averaging £6445) and like the rest of the prebendaries also enjoyed the fruits of those estates belonging to their stalls. Sometimes the sum was very small, but the archdeacon of Taunton admitted to an extra £100 and a further £450 when leases were renewed, and the archdeacon of Wells an extra £40 plus £75.

Wells cathedral was, it emerged, rather moderate in its income, but the obvious poverty of some bishoprics and parishes made a more equitable division of wealth essential and under the Cathedrals Act of 1840 that wealth was gradually transferred to the Ecclesiastical (now Church) Commissioners. The number of paid canons and prebendaries was eventually reduced to five as death or resignation allowed. The names of the prebends were kept and continue to be proudly borne by senior clergy (and now laity) as a strictly honorary mark of their roles in cathedral and diocese. Frederick Beadon was the last of the paid prebendaries: he was appointed by his father first to the prebend of Warminster in 1807 and then to that of Compton Bishop in 1809, became a residentiary canon in 1812 and chancellor in 1823 and held the last three appointments until his death in 1879 at the age of 101. Those prebendaries, coming to the cathedral without the ancient endowment as a result of all that change, were described at the time graphically if a little cruelly by Professor E A Freeman of Wookey as 'discharged canons'.

The cathedral, thanks to the initiatives of deans Goodenough and Jenkyns and the great interest of Canon H W Barnard (Frederick Beadon's nephew), joined the churches of the diocese in visible restoration of its fabric, and under deans Johnson and Plumptre rather more slowly in the revival of its worship. The building whose walls were covered in monuments, its fine stonework under layers of whitewash or paint, the bishop's throne masquerading as green marble and the whole quire an undisciplined jumble of plain and crowded woodwork, through Anthony Salvin, Thomas Willement and Benjamin Ferrey, was gradually revealed in its original splendour.

And against that visual improvement the chapter was inspired to restore the cathedral to its original purpose as a place of prayer. Deans Jenkyns and Johnson were personally against the innovations of the Oxford Movement, which must have brought tensions in chapter when Archdeacon Denison was present, though Jenkyns added some dignity to the services by making clergy and choir come to their places in procession. Hymns were sung occasionally from the late 1860s and in the 1870s weekly celebrations of communion were introduced. But still when Dean Johnson died in 1881 it was the high church view that any change in the services would be an improvement and the quality of preaching was particularly poor. Yet the theological college, housed in the cathedral's buildings and worshipping in the lady chapel, had added appreciably to the cathedral's corporate life, and the revived cathedral school also played its part.

Dean Plumptre, dean 1881-91, biographer of Bishop Ken and hymn-writer, introduced the cathedral to the Oxford Movement - white altar frontals, jewelled crosses and the observance of festivals and red letter days. Special services were held in the nave where an altar was introduced. Of particular note were the August Sunday evening services there for working men. The cathedral recognised it had both a congregation and a mission.

'PAROCHIAL IMPROVEMENTS'

In 1830 the young George Bodley Warren of Dulverton was curate of adjoining Brushford. His laconic diary entries record that almost every Sunday he 'served Brushford twice'. There is no mention of sermons either being prepared or delivered. 'Sacrament' was celebrated on Easter Sunday, Trinity Sunday, the Sunday nearest Michaelmas and presumably at Christmas, that year a Saturday when there was one service at Brushford and two on the next day. He noted that he took the sacrament to the elderly and the sick, that there were four private baptisms, and one at the parish church on a Wednesday. One Sunday he took the two regular services, baptised, and conducted a funeral. He churched one woman at Brushford, another at Dulverton, married a couple at Dulverton, buried two adults and two infants and when asked cancelled one of his services at Brushford to help at Skilgate, Morebath, Oakford and East Anstey. Once he attended a meeting of the Dulverton book club and said prayers, and once he attended the bishop's visitation at Dunster. For the rest he walked in the countryside, regularly visited a small circle of friends of his own class usually over tea, occasionally went to a party, 'stayed at home all day, busy', suffered from headaches, gardened (he had a passion for geraniums and auriculas), fished, played cricket, coursed hares, shot rooks, hunted stags, and noted every change in the weather. The diary for 1831 was much the same, but there was a new school to be concerned with, and the theft of Dulverton's church plate was a matter for great concern.

In 1840 services at Huish Episcopi were held either at 11 o'clock in the morning or at 2.30 in the afternoon by one of the two curates who served there and at Langport. In March that year the two congregations contributed 63 candidates to the tally of about 345 confirmed by Bishop Law, who came with his chancellor and his secretary. In 1845 after a fire the Langport folk attended services at Huish on the second Sunday in Lent in the morning and Huish people came in the afternoon; at Easter Huish people had the sacrament on Good Friday, Langport people on Easter Day. On Trinity Sunday they appear to have come together in the presence of members of Langport corporation and the alms amounted to £1 10s 6d (£1.52).

In 1845 'Churchgoer' (a Bristol newspaper editor looking to increase his circulation rather than seeking to improve worship) found great variety in the parishes of North Somerset. The new building at Easton in Gordano was 'cold, starving, comfortless, bare and barn-like', and at Bleadon the worshippers were few and the worship cold. Blagdon church had pews so high only tall people could see over them and the clergy hid themselves behind curtains. The music at Butcombe was provided by 'a great fiddle and a flute, and some singers, who did their best', the children at Pensford sang 'with simple but most sweet and effective melody', but a man with a bassoon discouraged the congregation from joining in at Easton. The rector of Lympsham not only read the service and preached (for 1½ hours) but led the singing and the chanting without support from an organ. The evening psalms at Portishead were given out by the rector, 'who read them through well, though with the slightest smack of what Mrs Siddons calls the "provincial te-ti-tum" ... a great improvement on the old system of allowing the parish clerk to perform the duty ...Portishead has not yet attained to that almost invariable appurtenance to watering places, a popular curate - a kind of public depository for silver teapots and embroidered slippers ... the vicar read prayers and reads well, though his endeavour to do so was a little too manifest'.

'Churchgoer' described the service at Blagdon as read in a way 'more singular than correct', at Publow and Pensford 'reverentially performed', at Keynsham with 'seeming lassitude'. At Yatton the vicar spoke at such a rate that the congregation lost their places and put down their prayer books. Sermons were 'neat' at Wrington, 'capital, earnest and persuasive' at Weston super Mare, abounding in 'pastoral illustrations' at Long Ashton. At Yatton the sermon was spoken as fast as the service, but 'Churchgoer' was obliged to admit that 'morning, evening and midday' the vicar taught, visited and performed acts of charity.

In 1855 came the death of Charles Francis Bampfylde, rector of Hardington with Hemington since 1814 and rector of Dunkerton since 1820, one of a fast-dwindling band of men hardly

Rebuilt in 1859 after Bampfylde's neglect: Dunkerton church.
Robert Dunning

fitted to the parochial ministry. He held the two parishes thanks to his father, the dreadful Lord Poltimore, and to the law that permitted him to have both because they were only five miles apart and he could with a clear conscience offer each one Sunday service. After some years he decided that Bath was a better place to live than either of his parishes, so he left them under the care of two curates. One of his clerical neighbours called him 'the most worthless fellow in the West of England' and twenty years after his death he was still remembered as 'the Devil of Dunkerton'.

W J E Bennett came to Frome at the invitation of the patron, the fourth marquess of Bath, while Bampfylde was still alive. He came from the parish of St Barnabas, Pimlico, with the opinion of the bishop of London ringing in his ears that he was 'unfit to hold a living in the English Church'. A leading light in the Oxford Movement, he rebuilt a collapsing church and introduced in it a style of worship including daily mass closely recollecting what had been practised there before the Reformation. When he died, still in post, at the age of 82 he left a parish administered through twelve visitors and rich in 'schools, classes, dispensary, provident clubs, soup kitchen and charities, a choir school, a home for factory girls and a creche for babies of working mothers'.

While Bennett was restoring at the heart of industrial Frome, the immensely rich Frederick Smith was building on a green-field site where working people of Taunton lived far from their parish church at Bishop's Hull. He began with a temporary iron mission church but in 1863 the church of St John the Evangelist was finished at a cost to Mr Smith of not much less than £10,000. All seats were free, the first in Taunton if not in the diocese; services were held twice on Sundays, twice during the week and on saints' days, but there was to be 'not too much gingerbread and tinsel', for Mr Smith said he was 'old fashioned', not caring for 'vestures and gestures'. At the opening service the bishop, Archdeacon Denison and the rural dean led about 70 clergy and a 30-strong choir.

Ten years after St John's was opened, Sydenham Hervey, son of the bishop, began his second curacy at South Petherton. Three services on Sunday formed the core of worship, with sacrament once a month, and other services on Wednesdays and, in Lent, Fridays. Hervey found his people thought a great deal about sermons and he had to lengthen those he had used before at Bridgwater. His duties included teaching in the boys' school, attending choir practice, running a night school during the winter and visiting, but he far preferred to be walking long distances in the neighbourhood, admiring views from hilltops, poking about in local churches or sitting on a gate reading history books. During the summer he relished early morning bathing in the river, cricket and croquet. Like his father an evangelical, he remarked on the fact that at a confirmation at Martock with 207 candidates all the clergy wore surplices, and the ancient chanting introduced by the high churchman V S S Coles at Shepton Beauchamp, he wrote, 'nearly drove me out of my mind'.

Ten years on again and the 'Parochial Improvements' recorded in the *Diocesan Kalendar* for

1888 were many and various. Including items from the second half of 1887 there were restorations and rebuilding at Axbridge, Brushford, Burnham, Chelvey, St Benignus' in Glastonbury, Queen Camel, St Decuman's, Twerton and Westbury, choir stalls for boys at Wrington, altar cloths at Broadway, Burnett, Taunton St John's and Wick St Lawrence, a cross on a superaltar at Ruishton, marble altar steps and an eagle lectern at Congresbury, an altarpiece at Charlinch, a reredos at Wilton, encaustic tiles at Dodington, stained glass at Dunkerton, retable candlesticks and vases at Kingston St Mary, and brass sconces, reading desks and other ornaments at Brompton Regis. Even the remotest parish had come a long way from the decency of a century before, revived in no small measure by the principles if not the practices of the Oxford Movement.

A clergyman writing in 1885 described the period before 1870 as one of general peace and goodwill with 'some temporary danger of lack of charity' as the blessings of peace after controversy came to be appreciated. After 1870 he considered that Lord Arthur Hervey had brought even greater harmony to the diocese and given it 'special characteristics' of union and order. By that time the societies that had done so much for education, church extension and clerical incomes, together known as the Bath and Wells Diocesan Societies and now under a single secretary, had joined with the Missionary Candidates Association (1859) and the Lay Helpers' Association (1882), providing training for work at home and abroad, to form the beginnings of a centralised administration. The year 1870 also saw the creation of the Diocesan Conference, planned to meet every three years alternating with similar meetings in each archdeaconry and rural deanery. The full conference comprised 180 clergy and 270 lay people with additional *ex officio* members. Its early result was thought to be 'general concord'. Not all were hopeful. V S S Coles of Shepton Beauchamp held a celebration of the Holy Communion 'on behalf of' its meeting in 1872, declaring in his diary that since it included non-communicants 'its possible influence for good and still more for evil make it an important subject for prayer'. Prayer was evidently answered to the extent that membership of the full conference henceforth was limited to communicants. The archdeaconry conference at Taunton in 1873 'went off peacefully' but Coles was not sure that such gatherings were of value and he found it 'difficult to realise what new ideas' had come from discussions. A ruri-decanal meeting at Ilminster in the same year, involving 20 clergy and laity, included, according to Sydenham Hervey, 'very desultory conversation on church finance' and a 'capital' paper on church bells.

11

I Will Arise and Go

Luke 15.18

In the ten years following the death of Lord Arthur Hervey in 1894 the church in the diocese was perhaps at its optimum strength, with at least one clergyman in every parish and mission halls and schoolrooms where on weekdays curates taught the working classes. The years before the First World War were also years of increasingly strident atheism, and clergy preaching 'God is on our side' found themselves without answers as the slaughter in the trenches became all too apparent. The vicar of Wilton wrote in his parish magazine in 1917 that private seats in church seemed 'contrary to the spirit of the times' but his new parochial church council was hardly representative of the working people of his parish. Nor yet was the church's new national assembly. In founding the monthly *Diocesan Gazette* in 1908 Bishop Kennion had wanted to reach all parts of the diocese with news of the church's activities, but it was unlikely to commend itself to the majority of those whom that same church had educated in village schools across the county. True, the issue of November 1918 included a prayer about the influenza epidemic, noted faculties for six memorial tablets and an item asking clergy to recommend candidates as pilots in the Royal Air Force, but nothing that could be described as recruitment for the army of Christ.

The peace that followed the end of the war was hardly enjoyed, for it was followed by economic depression, unemployment and growing international tension, culminating in the almost inevitable Second World War, further economic difficulty and an increasing loss of faith. Shortage of clergy and the money to support them brought a national report in 1964 that raised the whole question of whether the ancient parochial system was still the best way to minister in a fast-changing world or whether clergy (already at half strength in the country as a whole) might be deployed according to need. It also raised the questions of increased ministry of the laity and of the creation of groups of parishes.

In 1970 General Synod replaced the Church Assembly, and together with diocesan and

Opposite page:
I will arise and go.
Phil Day, 2004 (© Templar Trust)

deanery synods gave a more prominent role to the laity. In the first years of working, meaning-ful discussions were held and decisions were forwarded to the General Synod on the burning questions of the day: liturgical reform, union with Methodists and the ordination of women. The 1980s brought the culmination of long campaigns for a new prayer book (eventually emerging as Common Worship in 2000) and for women deacons and priests (the first in the diocese in 1987) but still there was slow progress on the historic status of clergy.

Alongside all those challenges was another, the imperative for all the churches in the country to come closer together for they are, in terms of statistics, a minority interest often unable to demonstrate their relevance to what is a secular society. Their members, in private at least, worry about its future viability and rejoice at even the slightest sign of increase in numbers. And yet in the growing popularity of cathedrals and in overflowing churches at Christmas, Mothering Sunday, Remembrance Sunday and Christingle services there is demonstrated a need in both young and old for spiritual contact and meaning. Similarly, the popularity of church schools is a clear indication that the work in education begun in the early nineteenth century, in spite of closures of small village schools, still answers a deep need in parents, and schools find themselves as effective as many parish churches in offering the Christian faith to children and young people. And different patterns of worship, away from Sundays and often more than a little informal, seem to be pointing the way to a revived and more relevant church.

There was something very new about George Wyndham Kennion, appointed on the death of Lord Arthur Hervey in 1894. He was only the second diocesan bishop in England to have been trans-lated from the colonies, where he had been a most energetic bishop of Adelaide since 1882. Before that he had been an equally energetic parish priest in the industrial north of England. He came to Wells when many of Hervey's initiatives such as the diocesan and ruri-decanal conferences, the Lay Helpers' Association, the diocesan branch of the Church Defence League, and the paid inspec-tors of religious education were beginning to make their mark; and at a time, in spite of harsh words from nonconformists about tithes and church rates, when attendance at church was prob-ably at its greatest. He was bishop here, too, when the national church celebrated the 1300th anniversary of the coming of St Augustine to Canterbury and the 1000th anniversary of the foun-dation of his diocese, the highlight of which happily took place in the restored ruins of Glaston-bury Abbey, the object of his most spectacular triumph, their purchase for the church.

But Kennion presided over little short of a revolution in the way the work of the diocese was organised and paid for; and he bore the burden of leadership during the whole of the First World War and its immediate aftermath. The confident hopes of a quick victory in a just cause

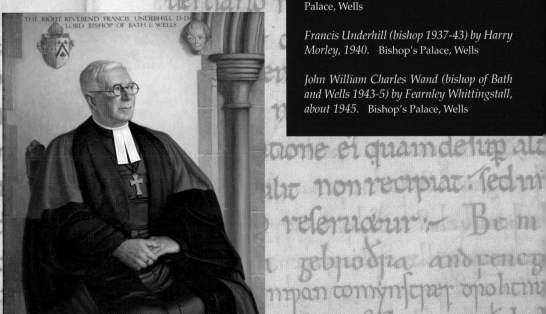

Clockwise from top left:

George Wyndham Kennion (bishop of Bath and Wells 1894-1921) by Wilfred Gabriel de Glehn, 1908. Bishop's Palace, Wells

St John Basil Wynne Willson (bishop 1921-37) by Adrian Savage, about 1930. Bishop's Palace, Wells

Francis Underhill (bishop 1937-43) by Harry Morley, 1940. Bishop's Palace, Wells

John William Charles Wand (bishop of Bath and Wells 1943-5) by Fearnley Whittingstall, about 1945. Bishop's Palace, Wells

were soon followed by wholesale slaughter and devastation on both sides, and speakers for the national Mission of Repentance and Hope came to the diocese urging the creation of 'a better England' when peace finally came. Hearers of a traditional kind were alarmed that women were among the mission's speakers and they formed the overwhelming majority in the diocesan conference just before the armistice that decided 'Germany must pay'. Kennion's private view is not known.

His successor after his resignation in 1921 was St John Basil Wynne Willson who, before holding the deanery of Bristol, had been a teacher and headmaster at three public schools for nearly thirty years. A former cathedral chorister and diocesan employee remembered his generous hospitality at the palace (made possible by his wife's income) and his addiction to golf with partners prepared to let him win. During Wynne Willson's time the church's newly-created parliament, the Church Assembly, flexed its muscles and produced a revised prayer book thought to be more attractive to modern tastes. The Westminster parliament rejected the idea, though the bishop made no objections to its quiet introduction in many parishes. And the national background of economic difficulty had its local effect in the poor incomes and large houses suffered by many country clergy, though the bishop could not induce small parishes to join with their neighbours to make better use of resources.

Wynne Willson's successor Francis Underhill came to Somerset in 1937 from Rochester where he had been dean. The Second World War involved the diocese first with hundreds of evacuees (including girls from a Bristol school who occupied part of the bishop's home and more who occupied the west cloister of the cathedral), then heavy bombing in Bath, and finally at the heart of huge military concentrations in preparation for the invasion of France. The bishop, so far as his health and petrol rationing permitted, was at the centre of action for support of so many people far from their homes and, in the face of widespread criticism of the church, organised councils of Christian witness across the diocese to discover what role it might play in social reconstruction when war was over. His successor described him as one of the unsung heroes of the war.

Bishop Underhill died at the beginning of 1943 while the end seemed far away and later in that year Wells received its second Australian diocesan in the person of William Wand, formerly archbishop of Brisbane, historian and theologian. He stayed all too briefly (though he managed to move the girls' dormitory from the long gallery of the palace) for he was involved in a sort of episcopal musical chairs that saw Geoffrey Fisher move from London to Canterbury on the unexpected death of Archbishop Temple; Wand took Fisher's place.

Harold Bradfield came in 1945 from Canterbury diocese where he had been at the heart of its administration for ten years and more as secretary of the Canterbury diocesan board of finance. Changes in the administration at Wells indicate his hand, but he was less successful in producing any plan that would ensure that all clergy were both fully occupied and at least adequately paid.

Senior clergy still remember Bishop Bradfield with great respect and admiration as a caring pastor, though at least one recalls a terrifying interview where the bishop's face was entirely hidden as he sat with his back to his huge study window.

Bishop Bradfield died in office and his successor was Edward Barry Henderson. He came with parish experience in West London and Scotland (where as a wartime chaplain he had won the DSC) and five years as bishop of Tewkesbury. He floated the idea of using his second name for his official signature but a rather traditional staff member in the registry persuaded him otherwise; in his later years in office he was widely and affectionately known as Bishop Jock. During his time one clergyman achieved more than local notoriety and one of his archdeacons rightly described his role as that of a fireguard that keeps the heat from the bishop. That same archdeacon was amazed to be offered promotion on the day after winning a heated argument with Bishop Jock in committee. More than once the bishop gave thanks for the fact that there were three race-courses in his diocese, and at least one priest in Bath was surprised and delighted when Bishop Jock (then just retired) appeared unannounced at his door and urged him to take the afternoon off so they could enjoy the races together. Rowing small boats on the palace moat recalled his naval days. Such apparent frivolity came amid perhaps the most serious and far-reaching work of the century, a commission chaired by Archdeacon Tom Baker of Bath (later to be dean of Worcester) that produced a comprehensive strategy for parish re-organisation - familiarly known from its cover as the Yellow Peril.

John Bickersteth came to Wells in 1975 from the diocese of Liverpool where a tradesman directed to his house when he first arrived there thought that the Bishop of Warrington was the name of a pub. His appointment to the ancient and curious post of Clerk of the Closet involved him in recommending the appointments of royal chaplains and in explaining the niceties of yet another prayer book, the Alternative Service Book, to Her Majesty The Queen. In the diocese he warmly supported the cathedral West Front Appeal and in a campaign known as The Standard tried to convince church members to support their parish churches more generously. Under him, in memory of Bishop Jack Cunningham, formerly bishop of Central Zambia, a link was forged with the dioceses of Zambia that is still a reality. Bishop John's fondness for shooting made him the butt of a cartoonist when the wildfowl on the palace moat were thought to need culling.

George Carey, principal of Trinity college, Bristol, came in 1987, and in company with the then bishop of Taunton, Nigel McCulloch, made a great impression as they led their Changing Lives campaign throughout the diocese as part of the Decade of Evangelism. He was, however, here but briefly and in 1991 became archbishop of Canterbury, the sixth bishop of the diocese to be so promoted. His successor James (Jim) Thompson had been bishop of Stepney for 13 years, kept from a diocesan post by Margaret Thatcher's refusal to promote the man who had told her the truth about urban problems in the Faith in the City report. His was the well-known voice that

Clockwise from top left:

Harold William Bradfield (bishop 1946-60) by Henry Raeburn Dobson, 1954. Bishop's Palace, Wells

John Monier Bickersteth (bishop of Bath and Wells 1975-87) by Humphrey Ocean, 1983. Bishop's Palace, Wells

Edward Barry Henderson (bishop of Bath and Wells 1960-75) by George J D Bruce, about 1970. Bishop's Palace, Wells

spoke the 'Thought for the Day' from Somerset for ten years from 1991 and that moved so many on the morning after 9/11. Peter Price came in 2002 from Southwark diocese, where he had been bishop of Kingston and before that general secretary of the United Society for the Propagation of the Gospel. In 1999 he was awarded the Coventry Cross of Nails for his work in reconciliation, particularly in Northern Ireland, Latin America and Iraq and is a passionate author, broadcaster and speaker on justice and peace.

✠ ✠ ✠

Bishop Kennion used the *Diocesan Gazette* in part to offer some idea of his activities. There is no mention of the time he spent at his desk in study and correspondence or in his chapel for personal prayer; of time in discussions with his chaplains, his suffragan, his archdeacons, of interviews with ordinands or clergy; of retreat or holiday. It is, on the whole, a record of his public appearances in and near his diocese. It is the year 1918, the end of the First World War, a time of leisurely travel usually by rail, of communications mostly by letter:

Thursday Nov	*7*	*Institution of a clergyman into his new parish*
Friday	*8*	*Higher Religious Education committee 11.30 [venue not given]*
Sunday	*10*	*St Mark's, Lyncombe*
Saturday	*16*	*To Taunton*
Sunday	*17*	*Taunton, St Andrew's*
Saturday	*23*	*Wells, National Society [education], 3 pm*
Sunday	*24*	*Portishead, Nautical School, confirmation*
		Ham Green Sanatorium, confirmation
Monday	*25*	*Bristol, National Nautical School, meeting*
Tuesday	*26*	
to		*London, Representative Church Council*
Thursday	*28*	

There is probably no typical week in any bishop's diary, but a week in Bishop Peter Price's diary will find echoes in those of his contemporaries, modified by the fact that he runs a joint office with the bishop of Taunton, sharing secretarial support and chaplains. At home Bishop Peter Price tries to balance seeing people in Wells with a programme of getting out and about. Although people think of a bishop as leading large services in church, he believes it is vital to get to meet people in the community. He is also a pastor to the clergy, and he tries to see them on their home ground whenever possible. The heavy load of preaching and teaching requires preparation time that can be hard to find. Three times a year Bishop Peter attends the House of Bishops residential meetings, which may be in London, the Midlands or York. Twice a year he goes to the General Synod in London or York. The development plans for the Bishop's Palace have meant also meetings in London with the Church Commissioners and the Heritage Lottery Fund. The bishop goes on retreat every year, and most years makes a pilgrimage visit.

The following is a composite diary for a week, compiled by Bishop Peter's senior chaplain and adviser Prebendary Stephen Lynas:

Monday 8.15 *Morning prayer in the cathedral*

9.00 *Office team meeting: diary check, planning for visitors, hospitality arrangements, transport details*

9.30 *One-to-one with archdeacon of Taunton: monthly meeting to look at issues affecting each archdeacon in depth*

11.00 *Journalist interview and photo in palace grounds: good publicity for the development is vital the help the public understand what is on offer to them*

12.00 *Senior chaplain: half an hour to deal with correspondence, pastoral issues, etc*

3.30 *Cathedral school to meet Countess of Wessex visiting the girl choristers*

6.00 *Leave for Bath ...*

7.00 *St Mark's school open evening: chance to meet teachers and parents and encourage work in this and other church secondary schools*
Back home around 9.30

Peter Bryan Price (bishop of Bath and Wells 2001-).

Tuesday 8.00 *Breakfast with Bishop's Staff and Sector Ministers: an informal chance to talk over what the various specialists at the Old Deanery are doing*

9.00 *Once a month all senior staff meet for a whole day beginning with Holy Communion in the palace chapel. Policy decisions are thrashed out, clergy and parish pastoral matters are reviewed and visiting speakers are listened to.*

5.15 *Cathedral evensong: the bishop welcomes and installs a new prebendary*

Wednesday 8.15 *Leave for Taunton*

9.15 *Address the Somerset Standing Advisory Council for Religious*

Education about Restorative Justice and the Changing Lives DVDs:
it is important to keep in touch with the education world
and show that the church is passionate about good education,
particularly in our church schools

2.00   *Back in the office: a vital half-hour with Margery, our*
Correspondence Secretary, and then with Caroline who organises
our diaries, followed by a planning meeting for the 1100th
anniversary programme in 2009

4.00   *Interview a Selection Conference candidate: all prospective*
ordinands have to be sponsored by a bishop.
Although our vocations team helps them through the selection
process, the bishop meets people at an early stage to find out more
about them and to start to form his own view about whether
they are truly called to the ordained ministry

6.00   *Leave for a confirmation service at Peasedown St John: one of the*
occasions when the bishop meets ordinary church members and
their families. Getting the service right is important, and so is the
meeting and greeting afterwards
Back home just after 10.00

Thursday   8.30   *Holy Communion in the bishop's chapel with the office team*

9.45   *A morning on palace business: the bishop is a member of the board*
of Palace Enterprises and a meeting of the palace trustees follows.
The bishop and his wife Dee are very active trustees. The palace is
owned by the Church Commissioners but it is vital that it pays
its way through tourism and conference activities. A separate
team has day- to-day management responsibility but the bishop
needs to keep abreast of what is happening - after all, it is his home, too.
Big developments are planned for the next few years

6.00   *The Bishop's Council meets after a sandwich supper: with the*
Diocesan Synod, the Bishop's Council is where the bishop meets
with clergy and lay people to plan and review the work of the church
in the diocese
Back home around 9.00

Friday   *Day off!*

George Leonard Carey (bishop of Bath and Wells 1987-91) by John Redvers, 1992. Bishop's Palace, Wells

Saturday		*Most Saturdays are quiet and give a chance for some reading, preparing sermons and talks or writing*
	11.00	*Licence new parish priest in village church, followed by buffet lunch with parishioners*
	7.30	*Supper with colleagues: a chance to be together and enjoy hospitality outside formal meetings*
Sunday	*9.15*	*Leave for 10.00 service at Witham Friary: it is a big occasion, their Patronal Festival*
		Drive directly to Cambridge to preach at Selwyn college's Evensong in their college chapel: part of being a bishop is to represent the gospel and the church to a wide range of people. That means travelling some distance.

The workload of a bishop has increased enormously since the 1950s, but the permanent help of a suffragan and the necessarily more temporary support of retired bishops has become essential; so, too, has become the role of full-time archdeacons. Charles Fane De Salis was appointed bishop of Taunton, the title first used in the mid sixteenth century, and he served from 1911 until 1930 when he was succeeded by George Hollis, formerly principal of Wells theological college. Harry Thomas, Mark Hodson, Frank West, Peter Nott, Nigel McCulloch, Richard Lewis, Will Stewart and Andrew Radford offered their different enthusiasms and insights in support of their diocesans, three moving on the become diocesans themselves and two dying tragically young with their ministries apparently unfulfilled. Peter Maurice, appointed in 2006, continues their tradition of inspired service.

Archdeacons are still the eyes, and ears, of the bishop and there is now far more to see and hear when church buildings are subject to exacting national standards, the behaviour of clergy and church members is under constant public scrutiny, and all at a time when financial and social pressures seem more often and more openly to challenge the church's purpose. The practice by which Bishop De Salis was also archdeacon of Taunton and his successor Bishop Hollis archdeacon of Wells may have suited the circumstances of the time. In the post-war years E A Cook could be both archdeacon and rector of Bath and his colleague Geoffrey Hilder could retain the rather less onerous vicarage of Hambridge and the directorship of the Moral Welfare movement in the diocese for a time when he was made archdeacon of Taunton in 1951. For fifteen remarkable years from 1955 he was also Prolocutor (chairman) of the clergy in Convocation and only in 1968 gave up his beloved Hambridge for a house in Stogumber and in his last days became a full-time archdeacon. Arthur Hopley, in 1962 Cook's successor as archdeacon of Bath and in 1971 Hilder's as archdeacon of Taunton, operated from former clergy houses first in Shoscombe and later in Angersleigh, but found himself, as did and do his successors, regularly on the road to Wells where they sit on many boards and committees and take on immense additional tasks. The bishop's legal team in a period of change played a crucial role, notably the chancellor of the diocese, George Newsom, and a succession of registrars beginning with C Wyndham Harris.

FROM AMATEURS TO PROFESSIONALS

Those boards and committees, brought together for the first time as the Diocesan Societies, are the direct descendants of the voluntary associations, societies and funds set up during the course of the nineteenth century to carry out some of the fundamental work that medieval bishops, in a much simpler age, managed to do almost single-handed. They were run for too long by clergy who also had parishes to care for and inadequate incomes, and by laymen with private means; and until almost the beginning of the First World War the whole diocesan administration depended on voluntary subscriptions and small endowments. So in 1908 the honorary secretaries of the diocesan societies and the diocesan conference, the inspectors of schools and the editors of the monthly *Diocesan Gazette* and of the annual *Diocesan Directory* were all clergymen, and the only lay professionals were the surveyors of clergy houses and other church property (called surveyors of dilapidations because they assessed the cost of repairs needed when a clergyman left a parish), the architect of the diocesan societies (responsible for church inspections), the chancellor of the diocese and the diocesan registrar. But by 1908 new societies and boards had been formed to provide for new needs and new challenges. There were four more with educational interests, one for mission, one for church workers, one for bell ringers, one for choral singing, all intimately concerned to improve and support the work of the clergy.

In 1912 came a huge change when most of that work came under the management of a single body, the diocesan board of finance, whose very name indicated the problem. Its work was carried out, inevitably, by committees or boards that still are the essential core of what is done at the Old Deanery a century later - finance, clergy training, property management, clergy pensions, church building and religious education. And there was in 1912 a new professionalism. Clergy still played a prominent part, but the chairman of the board was a financially astute layman, A E Eastwood, of Leigh Court, Angersleigh, a man who understood the financial needs of the church both local and national. He was himself both treasurer and secretary of his own church council and was in no doubt at all that his tiny parish, used to raising money for repairs through dinners, fairs, sales and dances, should at the same time contribute something to the needs of the diocese and to

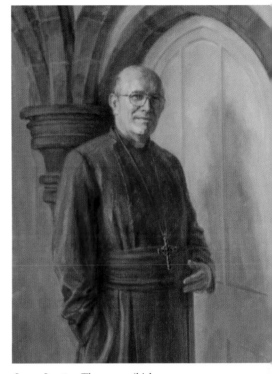

James Lawton Thompson (bishop of Bath and Wells 1991-2001) by June Mendoza, 2000-01) Bishop's Palace, Wells

the church as a whole. So Angersleigh was asked to raise the sum of £3 6s 1d (£3.30p) as its 'parish quota', which it met easily through a weekly freewill offering scheme and a special collection.

With the addition of a few more committees like the diocesan advisory committee (advising the chancellor on the granting of faculties) in 1921 and the diocesan board of patronage in 1932, the board of finance led by such influential men as Edmund Page and John Hayward continued Eastwood's work. Running in parallel was the diocesan conference that discussed the issues of the day as they affected the work of the church in the diocese. For years its honorary secretary was the hugely influential Canon J M Alcock, right-hand man to three bishops. He was domestic chaplain and private secretary to Kennion, Wynne Willson and Underhill from 1918 until 1942, was a member of the cathedral chapter from 1915 and before that was vicar of Godney and rural dean of Glastonbury. He was remembered for his incisive postcards: a clergyman indulging in too much newspaper correspondence would receive the message 'Shut up! JMA'. Canon Alcock knew more about the diocese than anyone.

In post-war Britain the need for social action by the diocese was pressing; so, too, was the need for a professional administrator working from Wells rather than Taunton. Thus it was that Arthur Butcher occupied an office, first in the Palace gatehouse and by 1949 in part of the Deanery, then still the home of Dean Malden. And when the dean retired in 1950 and his successor lived elsewhere the building became not only the diocesan office but also home to diocesan staff. Today, the Old Deanery is both offices and meeting-place. There are those who regard the people there as responsible for impossible financial demands on their parishes resulting from unnecessary expenditure. They do not fully understand that the shares assesssed on each parish towards the common fund pays for stipends, pension contributions, housing costs and on-going training of the clergy whose ministry has been the care and concern of our bishops from the beginning. In 2007 the sum needed was £7, 909, 290 from 25,609 members in 501 parishes. It was almost entirely paid.

THE CATHEDRAL

The prospect of having to organise a second coronation at Westminster is said to have brought Joseph Armitage Robinson back to his native Somerset as dean in 1911. He was a formidable scholar whose deep appreciation of the past was evident both in changes to the cathedral's services including the reintroduction of a processional cross and copes, but also in various improvements to the building. It was typical of him that the county's war memorial was not yet another stepped cross on Cathedral Green but instead was the restoration of two chapels in the south transept. Other similar chapels were similarly refurnished as places for private prayer, but his most significant contribution was the reappearance of the rood figures into the slots left empty on the inverted arches at the Reformation. The increasing numbers of visitors encouraged by the growing tourist literature of railway companies and motoring organisations were bound to be struck by that clear indication of the cathedral's essential purpose.

Dean Richard Malden, who came to Wells on Armitage Robinson's retirement to Upton Noble in 1933, was also a scholar and preacher and was moved during the Second World War to publish a small booklet in which he firmly restated that purpose, drawing clear distinctions between cathedrals whose histories reached back before the Reformation and those inadequately-staffed modern creations which he saw as little more than parish churches. For Malden the old cathedrals were 'the most splendid part of our national inheritance' representing 'the labour, piety, and generosity of some twelve generations of men ... the most conspicuous and most character-istic embodiment of the ideals and aspirations' of the times when they were built. But their prime purpose was the same as ever, to be places of prayer and praise to God, to be centres of 'sacred learning' and to be treasure-houses of sacred music.

Deans since Malden's time have continued with chapter colleagues to beautify and improve their inheritance: furnishings and statuary that add colour or focus attention. But age brings the need to restore and the great campaign led by Dean Patrick Mitchell (dean 1973-89) to restore the west front and the high vaults brought Wells to international notice both in its appeal for funds in 1976 and in its innovative techniques. A second campaign, driven by Richard Lewis (dean 1990-2003), was very much in the spirit of Bishop Bekynton in the mid fifteenth century in the way buildings for entirely practical purposes have been inserted within the existing envelope. Those who sing, teach, repair, maintain and offer hospitality can now operate in adequate modern spaces, leaving the cloister walks free from clutter and the visitor better welcomed, taught and refreshed.

Those visitors come in greater numbers as the appeal of heritage becomes ever more popular. The challenge to offer something more is also a great opportunity: a personal welcome, an informed guide, colour provided by flowers or shafts of sunlight through stained glass. Often furniture is being shifted or cables being laid in preparation for a choir or instrumentalists, for the cathedral is among the county's theatres. But it remains the chief church of the people of Somer-set that it has been from its beginnings; and remains, too, the place where faith is taught in the performance of worship or in formal lectures.

PARISH PRIESTS AND READERS

By the beginning of the twentieth century almost all our historic parishes had resident clergy, and just one or two, like Sock Dennis, had a rector but no parish and no church. New churches built in the last century in the growing towns were adequately staffed and an ample supply of assistant curates. In 1907 there were 640 full time parish clergy in the diocese, a rise from the 616 clergy in 491 benefices in 1887. They were joined, probably for the first time that year and mostly in mission halls and other unconsecrated buildings, by a few men from the ranks of the Lay Helpers whom Lord Arthur Hervey had recruited from 1881. Lay readers' licences forbade them to occupy pulpits but permitted them to say morning and evening prayer, and to read a suitable sermon or homily only if someone else more qualified had composed it. Five such lay readers had care of the corrugated iron mission chapel at Galmington in Wilton parish between 1910 and 1930.

Over the next thirty years the number of men offering themselves for the sacred ministry fell throughout the country, reflecting both a general loss of faith at least partly engendered by the First World War and the poor financial prospects, at a time of unemployment and depression. Lay readers, by contrast, increased in numbers: 62 in 1927, 69 in 1937. By 1947 the number had fallen to 43, but by 1956 there were 123 as compared with 454 full-time clergy all, of course, men. With the addition of retired active clergy, 800 men were offering ministry in the diocese. The first licensed woman lay reader, the remarkable Dorothy Daldy, was appointed in 1971 and by 1986 there were 255 readers of whom 31 were women. Deaconesses and other women parish workers were first listed in the *Diocesan Directory* for 1980/1. Women were first made deacons in the diocese by Bishop John Bickersteth in 1987. Twenty years later 192 men and 169 women readers supported 306 full- and part-time clergy, of whom 78 were women, and 232 retired priests. A total of 899 men and women were thus offering licensed ministry; but ministry in the name of Christ and his church is the responsibility of all 25,609 registered church members in the diocese.

CHANGING LIVES: CHANGING CHURCHES FOR CHANGING COMMUNITIES

The mission of the diocese at the beginning of the twenty-first century in response to the huge social changes of the time has at its heart that classic Anglican purpose to proclaim the gospel afresh in each generation. That was Bishop Lord Arthur Hervey's clear purpose as he moved constantly about the diocese at the end of the nineteenth century; that was Bishop George Carey's as he responded to the national Decade of Evangelism in the 1990s and Bishop Jim Thompson's as he encouraged all to 'Go For God'. 'Changing Lives' is the recurring purpose of the initiative taken by Bishop Peter Price and Bishop Andrew Radford that was officially adopted by the diocese in 2004. How to reach the current generation is the challenge that the wardens of Henstridge recognised when they planned to form a new choir to attract young people to church in the mid eighteenth century and Lord Arthur Hervey took up when he appointed a diocesan missioner in 1887. By different means and with differing emphases it was the challenge answered by Bishop John Stafford when he urged better teaching in the 1440s, by Bishop William of Bitton I when he demanded better order in the 1250s and by those who decided to create the diocese that is Bath and Wells in 909.

And change following challenge has in recent years been remarkable. The division of the administrative county of Somerset and the creation of Avon in 1974 recognised that the people of north Somerset had closer ties with Bristol than with Taunton. Subsequent changes have made Bath and Weston super Mare centres of administration, and the interest the diocese had in education and social services in a single authority had to be consequently modified. Those changes also recognised that the population of the north of the county was growing fast. The closure of the North Somerset coalfield in 1972 led to the closure of the parish churches of Writhlington, Clandown and Downside, but elsewhere in the area there was rapid growth. By the beginning of the twenty-first century the bulk of the diocesan population lives north of the Mendips: the diocese is no longer the rural one it once was, and the mobility of its inhabitants is a great challenge to evangelism.

The diocesan map from Freshford to Hawkridge, from east to west, is changing. Names like Athelney or Ivelchester appear from a real, and Camelot and Wheathill Priory from an imagined past; names like Six Pilgrims, Alfred Jewel, West Poldens, Postlebury or Fosse Trinity, difficult to find without an intimate knowledge of local history or geography. There are teams and groups and a few defiantly single parishes, their ministers called variously rector, vicar or priest in charge. Rural deaneries are still around but have been reshaped yet again and occasionally given new names, Yeovil replacing the elusive Merston, Sedgemoor the unpopular Bridgwater, but Crewkerne and Ilminster both kept, for both have an equally ancient missionary past. Now Local Ministry Groups are forming within deaneries, each eventually to find its own name and identity, to ensure that no priest need work in isolation and that scarce resources are shared.

That coming together in groups and teams is the inevitable consequence of shrinking resources from the 1930s and a dwindling supply of clergy felt acutely in the 1980s. Camelot (parishes around North Cadbury), Wellington, Central Weston and Yeovil led the way in 1975-6 in formal teams of four or more clergy, while by contrast the priest at Rode Major served five churches and might have recalled to some the galloping curates of the eighteenth century. Thirty years later, wonderfully-surviving retired clergy, readers and specialists in youth work, rural affairs and other ministries are partners with full-time clergy.

In terms of buildings used for regular worship, the landscape of the diocese has changed little. Eighteen churches and two church towers are in the care of the national Churches Conservation Trust - Cameley, Puxton, Langport, Thurlbear and the rest - and perhaps as many have been demolished (Crewkerne Christchurch, Wellington Holy Trinity) or like Wheathill, Curland or Gaer Hill converted to domestic or other uses. But flexibility is the order of the day for church buildings in current use, in some cases a return to days before they came to be seen as exclusively sacred spaces. For reasons quite different from those used in the 16th and 17th centuries and much nearer those moving the people of Dulverton to bring their reading desk closer to the congregation in 1762, nave altars often on moveable platforms have been placed in front of chancel steps. Elsewhere kitchens and other offices have been ingeniously installed and pews removed and sometimes replaced by chairs to create space for performance and social gathering. The activities of the late-medieval church house are back in the church.

Another near-revolution of the last 50 years is the changed relationship with other churches. The Church of England has been affected less by falling membership and clergy shortage than most others from whom for so long it was separated. Some churches began to work together for local reasons by the beginning of the twentieth century: a union mission in Ilminster belonged jointly to Congregationalists and Baptists in 1902. Methodists achieved nominal unity in the 1930s. Talks between Anglicans and Methodists eventually foundered in 1972 (the same year the English Congregationalists and the English Presbyterians came together as the United Reformed Church), but local councils of churches brought clergy and a few laity together in sometimes very effective demonstrations of Christian unity. Very practical cooperation came in the field of education demonstrated in shared Anglican-Methodist schools in Frome and Watchet, an Anglican-Roman Catholic comprehensive in Taunton and an ecumenical Anglican-Methodist primary in Worle.

Closer working in parishes is also formalised, for instance at Batheaston where Anglican vicar, Roman Catholic priest and Methodist minister share ministry with two readers. More spectacular is the new district of Locking Castle, formed in 1998 and named from a surviving monument to the Norman Conquest. A huge new community required a new pattern of ministry, at first headed by an Anglican priest but in 2008 still officially an Anglican area but led by a Baptist minister working with two Anglican readers, a Methodist and a URC minister. The formal details of the parish of Worle, also part of expanding Weston super Mare, read at first in the *Diocesan Directory* for 2008 like a typical urban parish of late Victorian England: a parish church, a daughter chapel and a mission hall; but the chapel is described as a community hall, the hall is a 'worship centre' with many other uses, and so is the old parish church. The staff list is far from Victorian: a rector, two vicars, a curate in training, three readers and a reader in training, a Methodist minister and an administrator.

▨ ▨ ▨

And what more shall I say? Here is a cloud of witnesses from the past who in their different ways and at different times 'enforced justice, received promises, stopped the mouths of lions'. Today's witnesses are all the people of God called into active discipleship and ministry, offered training for service in a School of Formation whose breadth of curriculum would have been the envy of the founders of Wells theological college. Changes in the way the diocese is governed are about to take effect designed to be more efficient and coordinated. The 1100th anniversary of the birth of the diocese is seen as an opportunity for mission. The purpose of the new *Diocesan Kalendar* that appeared in 1887 was to gather details of diocese, parishes and clergy together, for it was believed that such information would inspire 'that deeper interest ... for which the times that unmistakeably threaten us are certain to make solemn demand'. The times still threaten. This history of the past 1100 years is a record of many witnesses much tested and of times much threatened; may it also serve as a means of inspiring witnesses today and tomorrow.

Index